William Kingsford

Canadian Archaeology

An Essay

William Kingsford

Canadian Archaeology
An Essay

ISBN/EAN: 9783337186654

Printed in Europe, USA, Canada, Australia, Japan

Cover: Foto ©Andreas Hilbeck / pixelio.de

More available books at **www.hansebooks.com**

AN ESSAY.

BY

WILLIAM KINGSFORD.

MONTREAL:
WM. DRYSDALE & CO., 232 ST. JAMES STREET.
1886.

Entered according to Act of Parliament, in the year of our Lord one thousand eight hundred and eighty-six, by WM. DRYSDALE & Co., in the office of the Minister of Agriculture.

This Essay, in a different and a less extended form appeared in a Toronto newspaper last Autumn, with the disadvantage of having been divided into two parts with an interval of eighteen days between them. Much of the interest it might claim was lessened by this mode of publication. The present Essay has been entirely rewritten, and made to embrace a wider field of examination, and specially to include the consideration of the Archæology of the Provinces of Quebec and Ontario. It attempts to place in an accessible form much information scattered over many volumes, journals and MSS. Moreover, it brings to public notice the creation of the important public department of Archives, with some account of its establishment: a department by which the study of Canadian History must be greatly advanced, and any investigation of past events honestly and systematically directed. It is hoped that the information which the Essay attempts clearly to set forth may be not without advantage to the student of our Annals.

OTTAWA,   W. K.
    2nd January, 1886.

Ach Gott! die Kunst ist lang,
Und kurz ist unser Leben.
Mir wird, bei meinem kritischen Bestreben,
Doch oft um Kopf und Busen bang.
Wie schwer sind nicht die Mittel zu erwerben,
Durch die man zu den Quellen steigt!
Und eh' man nur den halben Weg erreicht
Musz wohl ein armer Teufel sterben.
                    GOETHE, Faust.

Ah me! but art is long
And human life is short.
Oft in the throes of critic thought
Have head and heart ceased to be strong.
How hard the means which in our effort lie
To reach the sources of what mortals know,
But ere a man can half the distance go
Verily, poor devil, must he die.

Your home born projects prove ever the best; they are so easy and familiar; they put too much learning in their things now-a-days.
                    BEN JOHNSON, Bartholomew Fair.

Ist das Licht das Eigenthum der Flamme, wo nicht gar des Kerzendochts? Ich enthalte mich jedes Urtheils über solche Frage, und freue mich nur darüber, dass Ihr dem armen Dochte, der sich brennend verzehrt, eine kleine Vergütung verwilligen wolt für sein groszes gemeinnütziges Beleuchtungsverdienst!
                    HEINE.

Is the light the property of the flame, if it in no way be of the taper wick? I abstain from any judgment over such a question, and I only rejoice that you are willing to make some slight amends to the poor wick, which consumes itself in burning, for its noble, universal, meritorious service of enlightenment!

Canadian Archæology.

Few are aware that in the last decade an important department has been formed in Ottawa, which in an indirect way will have no little influence on our political future. A people become to a great extent what their education makes them, and education in no small degree consists in the just appreciation of past experience. Certainly such is the process of political development. For however fascinating the narrative of history, the profit of its study lies in its teaching. There is but one mode of assuring historical truth, and that is by the collection of contemporary documents systematically arranged and kept in such security that they cannot be tampered with or destroyed.

Archæology is not an old and established science in the Dominion. Practically it can trace no remote date in the Province of Quebec. In Ontario it has had scarcely a quarter of a century of active life : in the Eastern Provinces it may claim a somewhat longer existence. But the study was confined to few, although there have been spasms of effort to deal with it satisfactorily and systematically. As early as 1787 the matter was repeatedly brought before the Council, and in 1790 an Ordinance was passed at Quebec for the preservation of ancient documents ; those which bore upon the French regime. A commission was appointed and a report made to Lord Dorchester on the subject ; a list of the *Decrets, Arrêts and Ordonnances* in existence was appended. The object in view appears to have been the preservation of all documents bearing upon the history of French Canada.

Little thought was then given to contemporary documents of the period, and it is precisely the epoch of which there is the least published record. The events of the first twenty years after the Conquest are even to-day but mistily known. They are repeated as first narrated by writer after writer without examination; or they are somewhat modified by a running commentary to meet *a priori* conclusions and to aid the party views of those who make a prosperous *état* out of printed opinions. Possibly many have honestly believed all they express. They found admitted authorities with a ready-made collection of facts, and they had only to follow in the beaten track. Even where the sceptical spirit was aroused it became crushed or dormant from its want of exercise. The collection of original documents, like any other collection, is a matter of slow, careful, and systematic labour. In no place is there a greater division of positive work. The accumulation of a mass of any material, say money, and then theorize upwards or downwards as you will, is an art of itself requiring special capacity. When the effort is a collection of National Archives you have to establish what is required, what is indispensably necessary, to know where to seek for it, to take means to obtain it, and to be careful not to pay twice over for the same commodity. The second stage is to assort all this matter, to classify it, to place it in such a form and to give it such reference that on necessity immediately it can be found. The third condition is to draw up a calendar of it, to describe it, and in short to make it available to the ordinary inquirer. One, therefore, who sees a collection of any kind brought to the hammer feels a twinge of pain as he thinks of the enthusiasm, the sustained effort, the frequent sacrifices which have gathered it only by slow degrees. Among the many monuments of Imperial London none is so striking, so impressive, as the reading-room and library of the

British Museum, offering to view one of the largest known printed collections of books and pamphlets, accessible to the poorest and humblest inhabitant of the realm ; admission to the room being only contingent on good manners and decent conduct. It is from this great centre that much of the impetus of thought and intelligence is given, and the sentiment established as a matter of national faith that in large Provincial centres, a collection of books is as essential to the well-being of the people to raise them from mental degradation, superstition, and extravagance of thought, as the air they breathe, and the food they take to strengthen and refresh their bodies. There is no point on which history so much repeats itself as in the exhibition of that charlatanism which urges itself forward without a scruple, without truth, without principle. And as a community, or more properly perhaps to speak, the teachers of that community, have the training and the knowledge to bring past examples of this nefarious success before the world, so is there the greater or less certainty of men being warned against the viper, seeking to secure its nest in the national bosom.

The Historical Society of Quebec is deserving of honourable notice by the publication of many important documents from time to time issued by its members. It was formed in 1824. Lord Dalhousie, then Governor-General, took a prominent part in its establishment, and presided at the first meeting held on the 6th January at the Chateau of St. Louis, when the society was organized. There is an Historical Society of Montreal ; its fortunes appear, however, to have somewhat waned. It never reached the distinguished position of that of Quebec, which, undoubtedly, has made many valuable contributions to our history. But the best well-wisher and friend of the latter must acknowledge that its operations have been fitful and uncertain, and of late unimportant.

Moreover, its views and aims embraced general history. It was not a Canadian Historical Society, and in a social point of view wisely so. It was instituted in a time when railways were not even dreamed of. If in those days of rigorous winter some sanguine enthusiast had prophesied the power of steam* ; if he had foretold that a train would await the passenger, with a saloon heated to the attractive atmosphere of a drawing-room, with a lounge too easy for a practical and

---

(*) One of the earliest to express an opinion with regard to the influence of Railways on thought and life was Heinrich Heine. The following passage appears in Lutezia, Zweiter Theil, No. 57. Paris, 5 May, 1843 : —

The opening of the two new Railways, one of which takes us to Orleans, the other to Rouen, [75 and 84 miles : Translator] caused here a commotion with which each individual person sympathizes if he does not by chance stand on a chair of isolation. The whole population of Paris at this moment forms a chain by which one conveys to the other the electric shock. But while the great crowd, bewildered and confounded, stares upon the outward form of the immense motive power, an awe-creating dread takes possession of the thinker, such as we feel when the most prodigious, the most unheard-of event takes place, the consequences of which are impenetrable and not to be calculated. Simply we perceive that our whole existence is to be carried and hurled along on a new path ; that new relations, joys and vexations await us, and that the unknown, at once seducing and at the same time tormenting us, exercises over us a mysterious fascination. So must it have come upon the mind of our ancestors when America was dicovered, as the invention of gunpowder was announced by the first cannon shot, as the art of Printing sent forth to the world the first proof sheet of God's Word. The institution of Railways is again such a Providential event, which creates a new Revolution [*Umschwung*] to humanity, to change the colour and form of life. A new chapter in the world's history has commenced, and our generation may congratulate itself that it has happened in its time. What changes must now step in our modes of thought and action! Even the elementary ideas of time and space have become uncertain. Through the railway is space annihilated and time alone is left to us. Had we only wealth sufficient the last decently to destroy ! In three hours and a half we now reach Orleans, and in the same time we come to Rouen. What will come to pass

earnest student, with an *entourage* which courts rather conversation, flirting, or somnolency as the case may be, with all the etceteras of life: what a general titter of unbelief and of suppressed contempt would have passed through the auditory accustomed to hear with the demeanour of a stoic the most tedious, rambling paper which might date at any period since the event of the Mosaic cosmogony. The Historical Society filled a void in Quebec. Few left the city on a long journey during the winter. It was a matter of expense, even of suffering on a small scale, and certainly of privation. The attempt was then to give wings to the season of snow and long evenings. In Lower Canada of that date winter was held to begin on the 25th of November—*La Sainte Catherine!* It was considered that what snow fell on the mountains remained after that day. The season was accordingly inaugurated on that *fête* day by small parties assembled *pour faire la tire*, the poetic expression for molasses candy, which the initiated well know requires to be pulled and repulled till it be twisted into shape. In those halcyon days, when there was more simplicity of taste, good manners were held to be indispensable and slang was unknown. Accordingly, there was a genuine hospitality, which made Canadian society renowned for its true tone and high breeding. With youth, high spirits and polished manners these simple reunions furnished many a happy gathering and many a joyous laugh. A dance followed, and it was recognized that winter had commenced. One cannot always *faire la tire*, or dance, or dine, or sleigh, or—toboggan, although a class of in-

---

when the lines to Belgium and Germany are carried out, and connected with the lines of those lands! To me it is as if the mountains, and forests of every country advanced upon Paris. Already I scent the perfume of the German linden, and the Nordsee dashes on the shingle before my door.

dividuals, male and female, are rising up in Montreal, who by their *outré* dress, manners, and conversation would convey the idea that it was the first, the last, and the most important duty of life. At that date, however, the exhibitions of female costume were at least restrained at daylight. The consequence was that the Historical Society was an admitted necessity. It was a creation of the condition of events, and it became replete with life and being. It still exists, but its old glories have departed. The literary world has no longer to acknowledge the obligations due to the publications made by the Society. An altered condition of events has given other fields for energy, and the study of the history of the country has again fallen into neglect and indifference. Consequently a few individuals have obtained command of the situation, and they have been enabled to lay down the law on many points bearing upon Canadian events, submissively to be followed by no few young men more desirous of obtaining reputation and prominence with as little effort as possible, than calmly and impartially to relate the events which they claim to record. The study of original authorities, except with some rare instances, has been passing away and responsibility is avoided by advancing the name of some previous writer, who, however industrious and respectable, in reality simply represents his own labours and inquiries.

It is mere commonplace to point out that every country acts with but ordinary prudence and fulfils a simple duty, when it preserves its archives and the written materials for its history. So much depends on the fact that history be honestly and truthfully written. Much of our personal liberty of the present comes from the consideration of the past. We are never so wise as when we profit by the teaching of experience. Everything to be permanent must be slowly and gradually produced. Constitutions may be granted, but they can alone obtain strength from time and usage. They grow to maturity. Hence we require the means of studying their advancement, and we best watch the future by knowing perfectly the trials and difficulties of former days. History is rarely to be found in one consecutive narrative. According to the genius and objective nature of the chronicler, we have his view of past events and his deductions of their influence. But, on the other hand, there must ever be two classes of minds by which narrative is related. This difference may be briefly set forth as the expression of the tone of thought dictated by the sympathy of the writer. In every State there are constantly two parties, which are antagonistic in those principles which they accept as a theory of conduct : and as one is led by influences of family or teaching to join one side or the other, so insensibly his views, his feelings, and his mode of viewing events are formed, coloured and directed. When the sources of original information are accessible to all, no injury arises from this peculiarity of the human mind. Rather inquiry is stimulated by it, because some strong expression of individual or party sentiment leads to effort in the opposite direction. The subject comes step by step into the arena of examination, and the historical student who has the industry to seek out facts, pushes investigation into the remotest sources. So we finally obtain the whole mass of facts clearly and plainly submitted to our intelligence, and we can ourselves form our own theories and conclusions.

We have the results achieved by the Archive Branch before us in the reports issued by the Department of Agriculture, to which it is attached. These reports appeared in 1872-3-4, and in 1881-2-3-4. With the exception of 1874, which is drawn up by the Abbé Verrault, of Montreal, the remainder bear the name of Mr. Douglas Brymner, the Chief

Archivist, and certainly the result shows that if ever man was in the right place, it is so in this instance. The account of the origin of the department is here furnished us. In 1871 a petition was presented to Parliament calling attention to the subject, and pointing out that it would be advantageous to establish a system of preserving historical documents, in the mode adopted in Great Britain, France, and the United States. It passed through the usual course, with the result that the matter was referred to the Minister of Agriculture ; on his report a sum was voted by Parliament in 1872, and an Archivist appointed.

In limine, it is well to remark that there has been some extraordinary and inexplicable confusion on a very simple matter, and it should be corrected without the least delay. If rival Departments are blundering, or if there be a perversion of meaning of any regulation which on its face is self-explanatory, Parliament should set the matter right, although one would think an Order-in-Council would be sufficient. There is in each Department a departmental record room, and its duties ought in no way to clash with that of the Archives. In every department many letters are received and sent. In some of them, it may be said, parenthetically, they have been deliberately and ridiculously multiplied to give the Department an importance which it does not possess. As years pass on these documents increase, and the space appropriated becomes crowded. In such case the older papers are removed to the general record room of the Department. All these papers are indexed on their receipt and they are described at length in the Indexes of each particular office. If reference be necessary in after time to any special paper, it can be found with ease. It is plain that such a provision is necessary. But the moment that in the slightest way there is any departure from the limit arbitrarily imposed upon its duties, the office assuming the custody of other than its own papers becomes mischievous. No ordinary department has anything to do with ancient books, papers, and records. Its record room is simply a place of deposit for its own official papers until by lapse of time they can be allowed to take their place amongst the archives as historical papers accessible to investigation.

The historical records include all which are not purely departmental. They should be placed under one responsible head, in a fire-proof building, which under no circumstance should they be permitted to leave. The number of books defaced, lost, and even stolen from the Parliamentary library at Ottawa is a matter of notoriety. The Librarians are helpless to remedy it, for they are powerless. The national archives must be placed beyond the clutch of be he who he may.

Care should be taken that the law is enforced, that all historical documents be placed in a common centre never to be removed from it. It is in the Muniment room that any reference should take place. No rule should be more jealously enforced or more carefully protected against infraction.

No one should be permitted to take from the building under any pretext whatever a book, or paper, or pamphlet.

The collection was commenced in 1872. "The work" says the report pithily, "had to be begun *ab ovo*, not a single document of any description being in the room set apart for the custody of the Archives." The first successful attempt resulted in the receipt of the Canadian Military Correspondence of the Imperial War Office. It extends back a century, and numbers 200,000 documents, bound in 1,087 volumes; 197 volumes obtained elsewhere are by their side. The classification, the arrangement, and the editing of these documents, must indeed have been a formidable labour. Johnson in the full press of effort of his immortal work described a lexicographer as a harmless drudge. Did any of my readers ever busy him or herself with index-making? There requires one of two pressures to persevere in it: enthusiasm of a high order, which is unflagging, or the necessity of earning daily bread. And what is indexing to the separation of 200,000 letters, to be placed in cognate classes? Another important duty is the correspondence. Smith, representing that illustrious family, is reported as having in his custody all the papers bearing upon their past. The archivist commences with a timid appeal to obtain possession of them. They have passed to Jones, one of the sons-in-law. The latter has a high view of the *status* of the family into which he has married. He desires to stick to every shred of evidence of its dignity. And so it goes on. Finally they are obtained. Then come the classification, and preparing the calendar of them. And this duty appertains to all objects of interest, little or great, from a pamphlet to a collection of documents. The writer of a pamphlet has now the satisfaction that it will be placed on record. His labour will not pass away. It will not come like shadows, so depart. His effort will not have been quite in vain. A time will come when party interest will be powerless to make or unmake a reputation, or to suppress unpleasant facts. The secret motives of men will be laid bare. There will be juster views in the apportionment of distinction. The epitaphs of us all have one day to be written, and as we are prominent on life's scene or live in retirement, so is the circle of our judges of the future, narrow or wide. The hour unfailingly arrives when the great body of their countrymen have to pronounce on the career of those in prominent positions. Evidence comes forth from quarters where it was never looked for, and facts become known, of which it was believed all trace had been destroyed. Some reputations will rise superior to every accusation, to every taint cast upon them by venal writers. On the other hand, revelations will come to light with their long list of personal and political iniquities to confer undying disgrace on the perpetrators of them. This consolation, however, exists, that the men of worth and merit will live happily, in fame, if in life such was not their fate.

Mr. Brymner went on his mission to London, M. l'Abbé Verrault, the accomplished head of the Normal School at Montreal, than whom a more devoted student of Canadian history does not exist, went to Paris. The departments of state, the Colonial, the Foreign, the War Offices, the Board of Trade (formerly the office of the Lords Commissioners for Trade and Plantations), the Tower of London, the British Museum were searched by Mr. Brymner. Some difficulties at first arose with regard to copying documents. Regulations were enforced which limited the reference; judicious enough with regard to individuals, they can scarcely, with justice, be applied to the Dominion with four million people. After some correspondence these restrictions were to a great extent removed. The Public Record Office, for instance, had very definite rules. No papers between 1760 and 1802 could be examined without special permission. This regulation indeed is generally applied to all departments. In order to have these restrictions removed, Mr. Brymner submitted a memorandum through the High Commissioner, and on this representation an order was given by which information up to 1842 could be obtained. As one reads Mr. Brymner's Reports one must feel a better opinion of human nature. Possibly it was no little owing to his tact and judgment; but everybody appears to have received him in the kindest and most genial manner. In Paris, Mr.

Plunkett, since appointed Ambassador to Japan, was most obliging. He took a personal interest in the success of the work. Lord Lyons was absent. But Lord Grenville had done all that was necessary on the point of accrediting the Archivist. Mr. Marmette, of the Archive department, tells us how in Paris he was charmed with the French officials, M. de Rielle and M. Aval. Mr. Brymner gives us a long list of the eminent men in England and Scotland who aided him with advice, help and sympathy. He seems indeed to have found the touch of nature which makes the whole world kin. Why should not we chronicle their names here? Why should not the renown of their hospitable virtues cross the Atlantic? The Earl of Derby relaxed the strictest rules. Mr. Meade, of the Colonial Office, was unvaryingly courteous. Mr. Vincent, of the Royal Institution, offered his personal help in obtaining copies of documents. The distinguished Arabic scholar, Pascual de Gayangoz, "is happy to help us at Madrid in our researches," and so it goes on. [Page 16, Report 1883.] Independently of those above-mentioned there were M. Marshall, Bibliotheque National, Paris; Mr. W. Hardy, Deputy Keeper of Records; Mr. Alfred Kingston, Public Record Office; Mr. Garnet, Mr. Kensington, British Museum; Mr. Overall, Guildhall Library, London; Mr. Stair Agnew, Registrar General; Mr. T. Dixon, of the Register House, Edinburgh; Dr. Fraser, Deputy-Keeper of Records of Scotland.

Surely it will not be unpleasant for these gentlemen to learn that their kindness and expression of sympathy are known and appreciated throughout the Dominion, and that they may take from our heart all thankfulness.

But one comes to hold one's breath as we have to record the magnificence of the Master of the Rolls. He presented to the Dominion a full set of the State papers published by the Imperial Government—367 volumes—an act of munificence which needs only to be mentioned in order properly and worthily to be estimated.

Mr. Brymner visited the several Provinces in the hope of obtaining historical papers from public and private sources. In Montreal he discovered important documents in a damp vault where examination was a matter of difficulty. The papers at Quebec were in a cellar under the Court House. An objectionable temperature was accompanied by the risk of destruction by fire. Otherwise these documents had been carefully looked after, and there seems to have been some sense of responsibility as to their value. At Halifax the public papers had been systematically kept, and in good order. As late as 1864, 200 volumes of MSS. had been selected, arranged and bound. In 1869 a volume of Provincial documents was issued, bearing upon the establishment of Halifax under Cornwallis in 1749. Further, they contained original papers as to the continual French encroachments after the Peace of Utrecht, the siege of Beausejour, the expatriation of the Acadians in 1755 with the official correspondence from 1755 to the establishment of Responsible Government. It was at Halifax that the military papers from 1779 were deposited. Many are of great value. They constitute the military correspondence alluded to, transferred to the Archive Branch.

At Fredericton no papers of importance were found. At the Seminary of Quebec there are several important historical documents. They are, however, considered to be private property. There must be doubtless many valuable archives equally in the Seminary of Montreal. Ought not copies to be obtained of such as are of value?

In London Mr. Brymner commenced his investigation of the Hudson Bay Company's papers. In the Public Record

Office he found many of the French and English papers written badly and hard to master. His next visit was to the Record Room of the Tower. He came to the conclusion that the latter contained few papers appertaining to Canada of value.

At the War Office, amid an immense collection of returns, orders, requisitions for stores, states of strength, details of routine, outpost duty, and regimental every day life, there are many documents of positive historic value. They embrace a period from 1756 to 1856, which includes some of the principal and most striking events of Canadian history, being marked by the closing events of the Conquest, including the miserable proceedings at William Henry at the head of Lake George and the gross, glaring, blundering of Abercrombie at Ticonderoga. We there can penetrate the want of generalship and the miserable failure of Burgoyne, although these facts are well known, and the verdict of history has been long unmistakably pronounced. We gain likewise additional facts of the War of Independence, and the events of 1812. Among the memorials of the latter, in the Archives Office at Ottawa, is the letter written by General Brock a few hours before his death at Queenston Heights. No Canadian can look upon this paper without emotion. At the Public Record Office, where, as has been said, special examination was permitted through the intervention of the Colonial Office, the papers extend from the earliest period. In the British Museum Mr. Brymner found the Haldimand and Bouquet papers. The latter, a Swiss officer in the British service, played a marked part in the closing campaign on the Ohio. These papers extend from 1757 to 1765. Colonel Bouquet's name frequently appears in the histories of that date, and his career must be familiar to the readers of Parkman's two last volumes; and who has not read them?

Sir Frederick Haldimand, a Swiss by birth, was Governor of Canada from 1778 to 1784. When in 1763 Gage was transferred to New York, Burton, then Governor of Three Rivers, was removed to Montreal, and Haldimand took his place. In 1765 he proceeded to England. In 1766 we hear of him at Pensacola, Florida. In 1773 he returned to Canada, and on the retirement of Sir Guy Carleton, afterwards Lord Dorchester, he was appointed Governor of Canada, which office he held until 1784. The Haldimand papers consist of 232 volumes; the Bouquet papers of 34.

There are few portions of our history of which we are so ignorant as that of the years intervening between the Conquest and the passage of the Quebec Act in 1774, and of the further interval to the Constitutional Act of 1791, which divided the country into Upper and Lower Canada, and extended Representative Institutions to the two Provinces. The first years after the treaty of 1763, was a period of somewhat arbitrary and uncertain law; but there is every ground of belief that attempts were made in good faith to extend justice and equity to both the old and new subjects. There is no room for suspicion to detract from the personal honour, probity or ability of either Murray or Carleton. There is ground for belief that Burgoyne had no little to do with Carleton's retirement from the Government, and that the former endeavoured to throw much of the weight of his failure on the want of support he had received from Quebec. The subject is too intricate to enter into in this place. Burgoyne himself, agreeable, pleasant, witty, unexceptionable as a man upon town, with courage and resolution to make him an excellent *sabreur*, or to fit him for the leader of a forlorn hope, was utterly deficient of all the qualities of a general. He was the last man to send as a leader of such an expedition which had its only chance of success with a careful, thoughtful man, of capacity, enterprise, and judgment, a born soldier. The one feature which redeems Burgoyne is his courage. The creek is still pointed out near Schuylerville, on the Upper Hudson, along the banks of which Burgoyne walked to arrange the terms of surrender with General Gates. He was scrupulously dressed as if to attend a royal levee, and he astonished the Provincial officers who were at the late breakfast given on the occasion, by his excellent appetite, and the perfect unconcern with which he accepted the situation; undoubtedly assumed, for he was vain, ambitious, and self-asserting, and must have felt keenly his defeat. Like all men of his class, he had every one to blame but his own want of conduct; and being a brother-in-law of my Lord Derby, a great supporter of the Royal pretensions, and coming within the shade of Royal favour, he could strike down better men than himself. It was after this campaign that Carleton retired, or was recalled. The Quebec Act of 1774 had then been passed. Quebec was governed by a Council to enact ordinances for Government, the inhabitants having authority to tax themselves for municipal purposes. Of the Canada from 1764 to 1790 there is a great deal to be learned. Much weight has been laid on the statements of Du Calvet, a French Protestant. The extent of the trustworthiness of his statements is a matter of doubt. He certainly was not marked by judgment, and his political views were by no means warranted by the situation of events. It is he who has principally given us our ideas of Haldimand. It must be recollected that Haldimand succeeded to the Government in a period of trial during the War of Independence with the States. We know something of these difficulties in the Memoirs of Madame Riedesel, and the Memoirs of her husband, the Major-General who commanded the Hessian troops in Burgoyne's expedition, by Max Von Eking. We learn from the lady that it had been represented to them that Haldimand was a man difficult to get along with, as nobody could please him. The lively little Baroness conveys the impression that he was an excellent person, kindly in nature, with a high sense of duty, and resolute in his purpose. Papet, a Hessian officer, speaks of His Excellency as one not fond of great formalities, but liking a good dinner, and ever ready to smoke a pipe with a friend. Another Brunswick officer describes him as one of the most deserving officers he ever knew. He built a house for himself in Quebec, and he commenced to form a garden about 1777. He may be mentioned as one of the earliest scientific gardeners and florists of the country. Madame Riedesel admired the garden greatly. In return, she tells us, for the civility she received she taught Haldimand, and the Canadians generally, how to pickle cucumbers. Subsequently, he built the house at Montmorency known as Haldimand House, the summer residence of Mr. Patterson Hall, yet in perfect condition; and, as in his day, still admired for its romantic situation, overlooking Montmorency Falls, and visited by so many travellers. Madame Riedesel conveys to us the most pleasant impressions of Haldimand, especially as she relates the manner in which he took leave of her and her husband.

In order to understand Haldimand's position we must remember that he was responsible to the British Crown for Canada at a most critical time. The failure of Burgoyne's expedition gave the death-stroke to further attempts by the valley of the Hudson. The struggle in Canada for the representative of British rule was really limited to keeping it British. Canada contained its sympathizers with the United States more or less, the principal of whom was Cazeau, who had money and influence. He managed to escape, a ruined man. Others are named in the same category, but who were not so fortunate. It was after the capitulation of Cornwallis, in 1781, that things looked blackest. No effort was spared to excite the Canadian population to join what was represented as the fortunate side, and placards were freely distributed declaring that English rule was at an end on the continent. The consequence was a system of espionage throughout the Province. Men suspected were watched. If they became or were considered mischievous, they were imprisoned. Haldimand felt that it was a time for no superabundant delicacy, and as he held power he exercised it. This fact is remembered better than any other part of his administration; and doubtless a great many arrests took place. Haldimand's duties were certainly marked by great difficulty. He had to preserve public tranquillity, and at the same time defend the Province from United States sympathizers within it. Haldimand's principal assailant, Du Calvet, had been engaged in the fur trade in the days of French domination. After the conquest he at once accepted British rule. It is on the writings of Du Calvet that the feeling against Haldimand has been created. There is more than probability that Du Calvet was even an active partisan of the Americans. He was certainly imprisoned for treason by Haldimand, and on this ground sued the latter in a court of law in England. Du Calvet may have been a patriot or an agitator. It rests for some dispassionate investigator to determine which. One of the difficulties under which Haldimand lived was that he seldom received news from the seat of war. The information which he could gather was only by means of spies.

No doubt a study of these volumes now being copied for the Canadian Archives, will give a totally different view of Haldimand's administration. One fact is undoubted, he was a man of unblemished personal honour.

One particular point involved in obscurity is known as the Walker affair. So far as can be made out, in 1764, no barracks being in existence, troops were quartered on the inhabitants of Montreal. A Captain Frazer, leaving his billet, a Captain Payne took possession of the rooms, by more or less of force, it would appear, against the protest of the landlord. Payne was notified that the rooms were let, but he would not give them up. The case came before Mr. Walker, a magistrate, who ordered Payne to leave the rooms, and on the latter declining to comply with the warrant, committed him for contempt. A writ of habeas corpus obtained Payne's release on bail. And now followed the proceeding which has more or less remained a mystery, with the additional doubt which it casts upon the character of the society at that date. Whoever dictated the proceeding, a number of individuals masked, with blackened faces, and otherwise disguised, forced themselves into Walker's dwelling, and personally chastised him so severely as to leave him unconscious. Several parties were arrested, among them some military men. None were punished. There are statements of the misconduct and insolence of the garrison which even now should be investigated. It may be looked for that the facts may be found in the papers which are being gathered. Murray spoke of the event as "that horrid affair." A strong reproof came from England, addressed to the Canadian garrisons. One Captain Disney, of the 44th, was tried; but his innocence was established—by an alibi. French Canadian writers state that Murray was recalled, owing to the feeling entertained against him by the military. It is to him we owe the first census. He records the population as 76,725, Indians included. He has left a remarkable letter on record, addressed to Lord Shelburne, dated 20th August, 1766. [Canadian Archives, Haldimand B. 8, p 1.]

It first was made more generally known by its publication in Lambert's Travels, 1814. Since that period it has almost been forgotten. He describes the British population at that date, a few half-pay officers excepted, as:—

"Traders, mechanics and publicans, who reside in the two towns of Quebec and Montreal. Most of them were followers of the army, of mean education, or soldiers disbanded at the reduction of the troops. All have their fortunes to make, and I fear few of them are solicitous about the means when the end can be obtained. I report them to be in general the most immoral collection of men I ever knew; of course, little calculated to make the new subjects enamoured with our laws, religion and customs, far less adapted to enforce these laws and to govern.

"On the other hand the Canadians, accustomed to arbitrary and a sort of military government, are a frugal, industrious, moral race of men, who from the just and mild treatment they met with from His Majesty's military officers, who ruled the country four years, until the establishment of civil government, had greatly got the better of the natural antipathy they had to their conquerors.

"They consist of a *noblesse* who are numerous, and who pique themselves much upon the antiquity of their families, their own military glory and that of their ancestors. The *noblesse* are seigneurs of the whole country, and though not rich, are in a situation, in that plentiful part of the world, where money is scarce and luxury still unknown, to support their dignity. The inhabitants, their *tenanciers*, who pay only an annual quit rent of about a dollar for one hundred acres, are at their ease and comfortable. They have been accustomed to respect and obey their *noblesse*, their tenures being military in the feudal manner. They have shared with them the dangers of the field, and natural affection has been increased in proportion to the calamities which have been common to both from the conquest of their country, as they have been taught to respect their superiors, and not yet intoxicated with the abuse of liberty, they are shocked at the insults which their *noblesse* and the King's officers have received from the English traders and lawyers since the civil Government took place.

It is natural to suppose they are jealous of their religion. They are very ignorant. It was the policy of the French Government to keep them so. Few or none can read. Printing was never permitted in Canada till we got possession of it. Their veneration for the priesthood is in proportion to that ignorance. It will probably decrease as they become enlightened. For the clergy there are very illiterate, and of mean birth, and as they are now debarred from supplies of ecclesiastics from France, that Order of men will become more and more contemptible, provided they are not exposed to persecution. . . . .

Disorders and divisions from the nature of things could not be avoided in attempting to establish the Civil Government in Canada, agreeable to my instructions. The same troops who conquered and governed the country four years remained in it. They were commanded by an officer, who by the civil establishment had been deprived of the government of half the Province, and who remained in every respect independent of the Civil Government.

Magistrates were to be made and juries to be composed from four hundred and fifty contemptible sutlers and traders. It is easy to conceive how the narrow ideas and ignorance of such men must offend any troops, more especially those who had so long governed them, and knew the meanness from which they had been elevated.

It would be very unreasonable to suppose that such men would not be intoxicated with the unexpected power put into their hands, and that they would not be eager to show how amply they possessed it. As there were no barracks in the country, the quartering the troops furnished perpetual opportunity of displaying their importance and rancour. The Canadian *noblesse* were hated because their birth and behaviour entitled them to respect, and the peasants were abhorred because they were saved from the oppression they were threatened with. The presentments of the Grand Jury at Quebec puts the truth of these remarks beyond a doubt, the silence of the King's servants to the Governor's remonstrance in consequence of these presentments though his secretary was sent home on purpose to expedite an explanation, contributed to encourage the disturbers of the peace.

The improper choice and the number of the civil officers sent over from England increased the disquietude of the colony. Instead of men of genius and untainted morals, the reverse were appointed to the most important offices, under whom it was impossible to communicate those impressions of the dignity of Government, by which alone mankind can be held together in society. The Judge pitched upon to conciliate the minds of seventy-five thousand foreigners to the laws and government of Great Britain, was taken from a gaol, entirely ignorant of Civil Law and the language of the people. The Attorney-General, with regard to the language, was not better qualified. The offices of the Secretary of the Province, Register, Clerk of the Council, Commissary of Stores and Provisions, Provost Marshal, &c., were given by patent to men of interest in England, who let them out to the best bidders, and so little considered the capacity of their representatives that not one of them understood the language of the natives. As no salary was annexed to these Patent places, the value of them depended upon the Fees, which, by my instructions, I was ordered to establish equal to those in the richest ancient Colonies. This heavy tax, and the rapacity of the English lawyers, was severely felt by the poor Canadians. But they patiently submitted; and though stimulated to dispute it by some of the licentious traders from New York, they cheerfully obeyed the Stamp Act, in hopes that their good behaviour would recommend them to the favour and protection of their Sovereign.

As the Council Books of the Province, and likewise my answers to the complaints made against my administration have been laid before your Lordship, it is needless, I presume, to say anything further on that subject than that I glory in having been accused of warmth and firmness in protecting the King's Canadian subjects, and of doing the utmost in my power to gain to my royal master the affections of that brave, hardy people, whose emigration, if ever it should happen, will be an irreparable loss to this Empire, to prevent which, I declare to your lordship, I would cheerfully submit to greater calumnies and indignities—if greater can be devised—than hitherto I had undergone."

We have crude ideas of this period. We know that what law was administered immediately after the conquest, was based on the Royal proclamation of 1763. The Admiralty law and English commercial law appear to have furnished the principles on which Justice was administered. There was great dissatisfaction. Accordingly deputations composed of British and French Canadians proceeded to the Imperial Centre, London, to complain of this unsatisfactory condition of things. The appeal to the Home Government led to the report of 4th April, 1766, by Yorke, afterwards Lord Hardwick, and DeGrey, afterwards Lord Walsingham. This fact must stand prominently out as a mark of the actual liberty enjoyed in Canada, and of the desire of the Imperial authorities to act generously and justly. At this date there was no talk of American independence. The proceeding could only have its source in the desire to establish a healthy system of government, and to make Canada prosperous and happy.

There is much to learn of these days. There can be no more interesting investigation than such a narrative written temperately and honestly; not to prove foregone conclusions, but to establish the real and true position taken towards the people of Canada, coming for the first time under British rule. Whatever faults there may have been in the system, whatever incompetence or misconduct on the part of individuals, so far as the known documents bear witness, it is established that the desire on the part of the Home authorities was to extend to the conquered Provinces sound and just principles of government. One point is indisputable: the immediate appreciation by the French Canadian population of the greater protection extended by the administration of English criminal law: although it has been said that the Seigneurs, with others of the higher class, accepted with repugnance the Jury system which extended jurisdiction over the lives and liberties of men in high rank to those hitherto considered in a humbler position. The main difficulties existed with regard to the laws bearing upon property and the undefined protection granted to civil rights. The litigous character of the French Canadian is well known. He has an abstract love of law, and is ready to have recourse to it on the slightest encouragement. There is no reason to think that this spirit was less active a century back than at present.

Montreal appears at this epoch to have been pre-eminent in the abuse of what was called the administration of Justice, in the exaction of unlawful fees, and in having a race of bailiffs who knew how to charge for their services. It is said that on each case heard, a demand was made for rent, for use of the Magistrate's rooms. It would be profitable precisely to know to what extent these assertions are based on fact. That the abuses in the administration of justice were serious is established. It is not equally certain to what extent the character of them has been exaggerated.

The limits of the Province of Quebec were defined in 1764. There had been disputes as to what constituted its extent. With the memory of the war just closed, it could not be looked for that the British Provinces would abandon their pretensions to territory which they had hitherto claimed and which had to be defined with regard to a conquered Province. The country from Ticonderoga to Crown Point and northward along Lake Champlain had fallen into their possession before the close of the war. Accordingly the southern boundary of Canada was established at the 45th parallel until it touches the St. Lawrence, which it was to follow westward. An examination of the discussions which led to this determination would still be of profit.

There is another doubtful point, which would repay examination. The attack on Fort Detroit in 1764 by Pontiac is well known. Pontiac hated England with an inexplicable intensity. The attack was foiled by the courage and determination of the garrison. The Indians abandoned further attempts on the Fort. Peace was made. During the contest 600 French Canadians were enlisted in the district of Quebec. Their sympathies were called forth by the danger of their compatriots of Detroit. When they arrived peace prevailed. It has been said that their services were ill requited. Was such or not the case? Hitherto, little evidence has been brought forward to sustain this half-made assertion.

The conviction is strongly forced upon all who in any way refer to original documents, that much of the history of Canada should be rewritten. The search of Mr. Brymner in bringing to notice the extraordinary letter of Charles I. 12 June, 1631, throws a perfectly new light on the restitution of Canada to France at that early period of its history.

Two years previously Champlain capitulated to Kirke. It is now established that the country was avowedly surrendered back by Charles, on condition that France would immediately pay him the one-half of the marriage portion of Henrietta Maria, which he had not received. It is hard to get over language of this character: "What wee chiefly understand to put in balance yf not in contract against the porceon money is the rendition of Quebec in Canada." We quote the letter to Sir Charles Wake, the English ambassador at Paris from the King. This letter is published at length in the Archive Report of 1884.

Of Kirke, who took Quebec, there have been strange misapprehensions. He is represented by French-Canadian writers as a renegade Frenchman. He was of an English family which still exists in Derbyshire. His father had commercial relations at Dieppe, and some of his children were born there. Kirke started from London, one of the merchant adventurers, with a patent of Charles I. Quebec was taken July, 1629, to be returned to France by the treaty of St. Germaine en Laye, 1632.

There is one point on which it is desirable to lay some stress, and at the same time express the hope that the matter will be thoroughly investigated, and that is the career of the French in Hudson Bay. Undoubtedly it is mixed up with much fable. One writer has followed the other, and we have ended by accepting as historical facts what are really matters of great doubt, and what certainly, in one instance, cannot possibly have happened. Charlevoix may be named as the authority for the assertion that Raddison and Des Grosseliers passed from Lake Superior to Hudson Bay in 1667. Charlevoix, like any other writer, is simply an authority for what came within his own knowledge and experience. What on the other hand, is narrative of a previous period, is only of value as it accords with the testimony bearing upon that period. A very little examination of dates will show that any such proceeding was simply an impossibility. If the journey was made it must have been by Michipicoten and Moose River. As early as 1641, the Jesuits, Jogues and Raymbault, were at the mouth of Lake Superior, but it was not till 1669 that the mission of the Sault St. Mary was established; that of La Pointe, the modern Bayfield, in 1670. Within the previous ten years the country about Lake Superior had been explored. The Jesuits' map was given to the world in 1671, and it is evident by the record of 1667, that at that date no white men had settled on Lake Superior. It was in 1665 that Tracy reached Canada; the date when the French Government commenced to take a direct part in its history. When he arrived the country was on the verge of ruin; its commerce had disappeared; its inhabitants, few and scattered as they were, were divided, and the country was so subject to the attacks of Indians, that the daily labourer going to work had to be guarded. In 1666, Tracy undertook his celebrated expedition against the Iroquois. It was not until 1668 that the mission of the Bay of Quinte, near Kingston, was commenced, and not until about 1680 that Du Luth constructed the Fort at the mouth of the Kaministiquia where Fort William now stands. The Jesuit relations extend from 1635 to 1672. No mention is made of any such expedition up the Michipicoten. Had there been such an expedition it could not have escaped their observation, and certainly it would not have passed out of their control. In 1669, Joliet was sent by Talon to explore Lake Superior for minerals. In 1673, in company with Marquette, he discovered the Mississippi. In 1682, LaSalle was sent out on his explorations, which on this occasion ended with the discovery of the Ohio, and during the whole of these events we hear nothing of a definite and detailed statement of this expedition from Lake Superior to James' Bay in 1667. Indeed, hazardous as it is to assert a negative, the remark may be ventured that it could never have taken place. The connection between Quebec and Hudson Bay at that date was solely by water, following the St. Lawrence, coasting Labrador, and entering Hudson's Straits. What French writers have been desirous of proving was that the French held possession of Hudson Bay prior to Gilham's voyage in 1667. It was not until 1686 that the party from Montreal under the Chevalier de Troyes attacked Fort Hayes, on Moose River. Never dreaming of an attack its sixteen inmates were in bed. The expedition proceeded thence to Fort Rupert to repeat the attack under like conditions. The whole affair was a surprise. The merit did not lie in taking the fort from a handful of men, but in the expedition itself, which was carried out through an untrod wilderness known in its main distance only to the Indian. It ascended the River Ottawa to its head waters, and crossing the height of land, followed the Abbitibi River to Hudson Bay. It called for endurance, valour, and determination of no ordinary character.

The Archives Report for 1883 contains, among many documents of value and interest, " Transactions between England and France relating to Hudson Bay, dated 1687." This paper is made public for the first time, having until now been buried in the Record Office, London.

The Treaty of 1686, by virtue of which these negotiations were carried on, has long been known, but not the Memorandum in question. The claims of England and France are elaborately set forth in statement, reply, rejoinder, and co-rejoinder. Every argument possible is adduced in the *réponse* of the French to give weight to their claim to the territory. No such claim is put forth as a discovery of Hudson Bay waters by the way of Lake Superior. The names of Raddison and DesGrosseliers are mentioned on three occasions certainly. No claim of such discovery by them is advanced, although their treason to French interests and their subsequent pardon are named. What the French did claim was that in 1656 Jean Bourbon sailed to Hudson Bay and took possession of it; that in 1661 Perè Dablon, with Sieur de la Vallière, with five soldiers, was sent back from Quebec with some Indians who had arrived from the Baye du Norde (presumably Hudson Bay) and planted a cross there; that in 1663 the Sieur Couture, with five men made the journey from Quebec to the Baye du Nord, and planted a cross. In 1671, however, St. Lusson, accompanied by Nicolas Perrot, as interpreter, went to Sault St. Mary to meet the Ottawa and Northern Indians to receive homage from them; in itself presumptive evidence that no overland journey previously had been made from Lake Superior. The document in question clearly establishes that at that date there was not even mention of a journey having been made in 1667 from Lake Superior to Hudson Bay by Raddisson and DesGrosseliers. This document is of great value, and requires to be carefully studied. Nothing appears to be known of the narratives of La Vallière and Couture. It is believed that this criticism is now made for the first time, and it is to be hoped that it will lead to a further investigation of the career of the French in Hudson Bay, much of which is given with exaggeration. We almost seem to be again wondering at the mythical labours of Hercules as we read the feats as they are recorded.

In thus having described the present satisfactory condition of our Canadian Archives, we must equally bear in mind that the early progress of the Province of Quebec in the path of Archæology claims honourable mention, and the inquirer will meet the names of many engaged in its study commanding respect and attention. Printing was simply unknown in the French régime, but it is an error to suppose that no effort was made for the education of the people. The fact is clearly established that special provision was made in Montreal for the education of school-masters. The Institution on which this duty was imposed ceased to exist about the date of the Conquest: *L'Hopital General*, and its place was taken by the *Sœurs Grises*. As early as 1718,* the *frères* Charon, so named after their founder, were held to nourish and instruct eight pupils as teachers, receiving a subsidy for that purpose from the French king. As these youth reached manhood they passed to the country parishes as school-masters, giving instruction gratuitously. Charlevoix† especially names the attainments

---

*Vide.—Arrêt du Conseil d'Etat du roi. Donné à Paris au mois de **Février 1718.** Quebec Edition, 1854, Vol I, page 390.

Et qu'il seroit très avantageux pour le **bien** du diocèse de Québec de pouvoir **former dans cet** hopital des maitres d'écoles pour **les** envoyer dans **les paroisses de la** campagne, étant d'ailleurs informé que les jeunes garçons **manquent d'instruction dans notre dite** colonie **de Canada** pendant que les jeunes **filles en** reçoivent **par** le moyen des Sœurs de la Congrégation qui sont établies dans la plus grande partie des cures de la campagne, nous avons résolu en confirmant l'établissement du dit hôpital d'autoriser particulièrement ceux qui le composent, et le composeront à l'avenir à l'instruction des jeunes garçons et de donner à cet hôpital un fonds pour l'entretien d'un certain nombre de maitres d'école.

†**Sans autre** ressource que son courage et sa **confiance en Dieu** elle [Marguerite **Bourgeois**] entreprit de procurer **à** toutes les jeunes personnes de son sexe, **quelque pauvres** et quelque abandonnées qu'elles fussent une éducation qui n'ont point dans les royaumes les plus policés, beaucoup de Filles même de condition ; et elle y a réussi au point qu'on

of the female portion of the community. The Edict establishing these school-masters, speaks of the girls being well cared for. The writer is informed by a reliable authority who has taken pains to examine into the matter, that at the beginning of the eighteenth century, the number of signatures to the registers of marriages and baptisms, taking the population relatively, is in excess of those which appeared ten years ago. A proof—so far as teaching, reading and writing—that these schools attained this result : that the majority of French-Canadians at an early date could read and write. With the higher classes it was obligatory to have some cultivation, even if the taste for letters did not exist ; certainly there is no trace in the correspondence of that date of any deficiency of this character, setting orthography aside, nor can one instance of incompetence and ignorance be remembered on the part of those who occupied high posi-

---

voit toujours avec un nouvel étonnement des femmes jusque dans le sein de l'indigence et de la misère parfaitement instruites de leur religion *qui n'ignorent rien de ce qu'elles doivent scavoir, pour s'occuper utilement dans leurs Familles* et qui par leurs manières, leur façon de s'exprimer et leur politesse, *ne le cèdent* point à celles qui parmi nous ont été élevées avec plus de soin. C'est la justice que rendent aux *Filles de la Congrégation* tous ceux qui ont fait quelque séjour en Canada.

    CHARLEVOIX, tome I, p. 343, Liv. VIII, [1659], Paris, 1744.

[The Italics are the writer's.]

While **on the subject of Canadian womanhood, under the French** *regime*, **it will not be inappropriate to repeat the remarks of Peter Kalm, who was in Canada in 1749. Kalm's sympathies were strongly with French feeling in every respect.**

"The difference between the manners and **customs of the French in** *Montreal* **and** *Canada*, **and those of the** *English* **in** the *American* **colonies is as great as that between the manners** of those two nations in *Europe*. The women in general are handsome here ; they are **wellbred and** virtuous, with an innocent and becoming freedom. They dress out very fine on Sundays, and though on the other days **they do** not take much pains with other parts of their dress, yet they **are very fond of adorning their heads, the hair of which is always curled and**

tions. Printing first took form after the Conquest. The *Quebec Gazette* was published 21st June, 1764. It was projected in Philadelphia by William Brown and Thomas Gilmore. The latter went to England to purchase type and press, the former came to Canada to obtain subscribers. Events, however, were not tending to create sympathy with education. The future was full of difficulty. The United States, as united Colonies, had learned the strength they possessed when acting together, and the public men were impatient of Imperial control. The Ministry in power in England,—it is a farce to call them statesmen,—seem in no way to have known the problem with which they had to deal. The crisis needed a delicate, if it called for a firm hand, and selection should have been made of the wisest and most experienced of public men to cope with the emergency.

---

powdered, and ornamented with glittering bodkins and aigrettes. Every day but Sunday they wear a little neat jacket, and a short petticoat which hardly reaches half the leg, and in this particular they seem to imitate the Indian women. The heels of their shoes are high and very narrow, and it is surprising how they walk on them. In their knowledge of economy they greatly surpass the English women in the plantations, who have indeed taken the liberty of throwing all the burden of housekeeping upon their husbands, and sit in their chairs all day with folded arms. The women on the contrary do not spare themselves, especially among the common people, where they are always in the fields, meadows, stables, &c., and do not dislike any work whatsoever. However, they seem rather remiss in regard to the cleaning of the utensils and apartments; for sometimes the floors both in the town and country were hardly cleaned once in six months, which is a disagreeable sight to one who comes from amongst the *Dutch* and *English*, where the constant scouring and scrubbing of the floors is reckoned as important as the exercise of religion itself. To prevent the thick dust which is thus left on the floor from being noxious to the health, the women wet it several times a day, which renders it more consistent, repeating the operation as often as the dust is dry and rises again. Upon the whole, however, they are not averse to

If any argument be needed to show how powerless Court control is to meet a national emergency, it is the reign of George III. Particularly in the early years of the reign, when Court favour alone traced the path to distinction. The Generals sent to the United States, are to-day remembered only by their professional incompetence, and their want of military capacity; the English Ministers by their obstinate folly and dreary ignorance of statesmanship. It may be remarked that the principles of Constitutional Colonial Government were unknown, that they had to be "learned by suffering." But the difficulties with the United States, in the first instance, could have been overcome by tact, forbearance and firmness so to influence the great mass of the

> the taking a part in all the business of housekeeping, and I have with pleasure seen the daughters of the better sort of people, and of the Governor himself, not too finely dressed, and going into kitchens and cellars to look that everything be done as it ought. Vol. II. pp. 224-5.
>
> All the women in the country, without exception, wear caps of some kind or other. Their jackets are short, and so are their petticoats, which scarce reach down to the middle of their legs; and they have a silver cross hanging down on the breast. In general, however, they are very laborious; however, I saw some who, like the *English* women in the colonies, did nothing but prattle all the day. When they have anything to do within doors they (especially the girls) commonly sing songs in which the words *amour* and *cœur* are very frequent. In the country it is usual that when the husband receives a visit from persons of rank, and dines with them, his wife stands behind and serves him; but in the towns the ladies are more distinguished, and would willingly assume an equal, if not a superior power to their husbands. When they go out of doors they wear long cloaks, which cover all their other clothes, and are either grey, brown or blue. The men sometimes make use of them when they are obliged to go in the rain. The women have the advantage of being in a *deshabille* under these cloaks without anybody's perceiving it. Vol. II. pp. 244-45.
>
> Travels into North America, &c., &c., by Peter Kalm. Translated by John Reinhold Forster. London, 1772.

people that they would not have been dupes to the special pleading of the men of the stamp of Jefferson, who were actuated more by personal ends than by patriotism. It was the blunders of the Home Government which gave these men strength. How can any of us in Canada to-day, without indignation, read the title of the monstrous Act of 1767 ? "For restraining the people of New York from passing any Act till they had complied with the Act of Parliament for the furnishing His Majesty's troops with the necessaries required by the Act : and for putting American duties into the hands of Commissioners." Before three years had expired the troops under Captain Preston had fired upon the mob in Boston, and three men had fallen dead. Canadian sympathy is in a marked degree against New York in this point of the quarrel. That Province refused to furnish barracks to the troops quartered there. How easy might this paltry difference have been accommodated with a little judgment and forbearance !

These events are alluded to, to show what influences were at work on the continent to direct men's minds to other views than the Arts of Peace. It is true that at this date news travelled slowly. But the communication passed by the same route as when Tracy chastised the Mohawks; by water from New York to Albany, thence along the banks of the Hudson to Fort Edward, and thence to Lake George. The portage was made to Ticonderoga, and Lake Champlain followed to Saint John's, for the road to be taken by Chambly to Longueuil. In 1783, peace was made, with the loss to Great Britain of the southern part of the continent.

It is easy to conceive that for the first thirty years after the Conquest, literature could take but slight root in a country passing through such an ordeal as Canada had to outlive. The early years of British rule were full of difficulty.

There cannot be a doubt that Murray's description of the early years of his government must be accepted as the truth. The problem of government was not only misunderstood but disregarded in the appointment of the first officials. But the grievous error of that day was certainly not long continued or repeated. The men who followed the first comers were not only marked by great ability, but they were distinguished by high personal character. Prominent among them may be mentioned Masères, Marriott* and Grant; and the early establishment of settled institutions by the Canada Act of 1774 is a proof of the earnest desire of the Imperial Government to establish an honest and able administration of affairs. It may be easily recognized how the whole ability of the country was turned to the consideration of the system of law, and of civil institutions which were to prevail.

---

*One of the earliest books after the conquest is "Plan of a Code of Laws for the Province of Quebec, reported by an Advocate General. London, 1774." It is the production of Mr. Marriott, Advocate General, and was published during the discussions which originated from the proposed passage of the Quebec Act. During the first years succeeding the conquest there was undoubtedly great difference of opinion with regard to the Code of Laws, and the principles of Government which should be followed in Canada. The difficulties which arose about this time in Boston, Philadelphia and New York, exercised no little influence on the legislation of the new Province. The Archives Report 1883, p. 9, alludes to this "Plan of a Code of Laws," and points out that several of the Law Reports of the Law officers of the Crown are missing in the volumes bearing upon Canadian History from the Conquest to 1774, at the same time suggesting that they may be found at the Privy Council Office. Mr. Brymner pertinently remarks, "As the various reports and other documents relate to the Quebec Act of 1774, it is very desirable that they should be all accessible here together with the other papers as bear upon the same subject." We are, however, acquainted with much of both Wedderburn's and Thurlow's Reports, extended extracts being given in Christie's History, vol. 1, pp. 43, 45, and pp. 46, 63.

The war of Independence followed to throw its gloom over Canada. The one thought then became to defend the country from aggression. The Peace of Versailles of 1783 first furnished breathing time to the Province. Material interests alone were thought of, and what mental activity was called into being, was entirely devoted to the consideration of the political requirements of the hour, the discussions concerning which, to some extent, were silenced by the Quebec Act of 1791.

In 1792, 17th December, the House of Assembly met for the first time in British America, and from that date the literary activity of Canada may be traced. The first production the writer has seen was the "*Quebec Magazine* or useful and entertaining Repository of Science, Morals, History, Politics, &c., particularly adapted for the use of British America, by a society of gentlemen in Quebec." The first number appeared 1792, 1st August. The last number seen by the writer is February, 1794. It forms three volumes, and was published by Samuel Neilson, Quebec.

Le Courier de Quebec appeared 3rd January, 1807, by Mr. Young, Quebec. It was published on Wednesdays and Saturdays. It is not known that it existed for more than half-a-year. One volume only has been met with.

Le Canadien belongs to this date. Its first number appeared on the 22nd November, 1806, the last, 14th March, 1810, when under warrant of Chief Justice Sewell a party of soldiers with a magistrate took possession of the printing office, presses, type and paper. It was suppressed. The printer and three members of the Assembly were arrested as the owners of a treasonable journal. The one arbitrary, unprovoked, discreditable act which is a stain on the escutcheon of British rule in Canada.

Mr. H. Mezière commenced *L'Abeille Canadienne Journal de Litterature et des Sciences*, 1st August, 1818.

Eight journals are spoken of by the editor at that date as being published in English and French in Canada.

They were as follow to the number of seven :—

Quebec Gazette,	established	21st June, 1764.
" Mercury,	"	5th January, 1805.
La Gazette de Trois Rivières,	"	12th August, 1817.
Montreal Gazette,	"	3rd August, 1795.
" Spectator,	"	1st June, 1813.
" Herald,	"	19th October, 1811.
" Aurore,	"	1st October, 1816.

The eighth must be left for the examination of the readers of this essay. No trace can be found of it, unless it be the *Abeille* itself.

Le Spectateur Canadien was published by Messrs. C. B. Pasteur & Co. The first number appeared on the 1st June, 1813, it was continued until 3rd February, 1821.

It has been said that the *Montreal Gazette* was first published in 1795. There were, however, two unsuccessful attempts to establish it ten years previously.

There does not appear any note when an English printing press was established in Montreal. "Bibaud Jeune," in his *Institutions de l'histoire* mentions French printing to have commenced in 1777,—the Gazette Litteraire* de Fleury Mesplet appeared in 1778.

The various journals and papers of Lower Canada are marked by the spirit of three epochs, into which the history of Canada is divided, viz. :—from the Conquest and settle-

---

*L'arrivée en Canada de M. Fleury Mesplet imprimeur Français qui avait exercé son art à Philadelphie fournit aux Canadiens l'occasion de faire voir qu'ils n'étaient pas aussi étrangers à la littérature et aux sciences, qu'on l'avaient cru ou feint de le croire. La proposition qu'il fit de publier une feuille hebdomadaire fut accueillie favorablement et le premier numéro de la *Gazette Littéraire* (pour la ville et le

ment of Government on the establishment of the new regime to the Constitutional Act of 1791 ; from this date until the events of 1837-38 and to the Union of 1841: thence to Confederation in 1867. Until the first meeting of the Legislature little can be traced of literary effort. *The Quebec Gazette* of 1764 is the one record remaining. From the date of Parliamentary Government there has been a continual increasing political and social literature. The first efforts are by no means petty or mean. They can be read to-day with profit. There are few volumes of that date published in any country superior to the Quebec Magazine of 1792. Its writers were men of education, and wrote with ability, and discretion. With a larger public it would have gained a support permanently to sustain it. It failed, not from want of ability, but from the narrow field of its circulation,

---

district de Montréal) parut le 3 juin 1778. Plusieurs des essais qui remplirent les colonnes de ce journal pendant la durée de sa publication qui fut d'une année font honneur au jugement et au bon goût de leurs auteurs.

BIBAUD, Histoire du Canada, II, p. 78.

The first book published in Canada is generally believed to be *Catéchisme du Diocèse de Sens imprimé à Quebec, chez Brown et Gilmour*, 1765. The latter were the proprietors of the *Quebec Gazette*. A copy was exhibited at the Caxton celebration, at Montreal, 26-29 June, 1877, by Mr. Justice Baby. The first book published in Montreal is supposed to be *Règlement de la Confrérie de l'Adoration Perpétuelle du Saint Sacrement et de la Bonne Mort, chez F. Mesplet et C. Berger*, *Montreal*, 1776. Three copies were exhibited at the Caxton Exhibition by the Numismatic Society of Montreal, by M. Latour and Mr. Sheriff Chauveau.

If the date be correct, there was a printing press in operation in 1776

The second book published in Canada has relation to the Walker affair, and the opinion is forced upon the student of our history, that the publication was dictated by the political exigencies of the period. The very title is suggestive of this theory. "The Trial of Daniel Desney, Esq., Captain of a company in His Majesty's 44th Regiment

that it could not possibly be remunerative. It will be felt by all who turn to these early productions that the tone in language, style and matter is really of a higher horizon than the general press writing of to-day. One curious production of a somewhat later date is the *Free Press*, published at Burlington, Vermont. It bears the name of Lewis Luke Macculloh. The first number was dated 10th October, 1822, —No. 47, 4th September, 1823,—No. 48, 24th June, 1824. It is believed that this number is the last.

Of the same character is the *Scribbler*. "A series of weekly Essays published in Montreal, L.C., on Literary, Critical, Satirical, Moral and Local subjects, interspersed with pieces

---

of Foot, and Town Major of the Garrison at Montreal, at the Session of the Supreme Court of Judicature holden at Montreal on Saturday, the 28th day of February, and thence continued by adjournments to Wednesday, the 11th day of March, 1767, before the Honourable William Hey, Esq., Chief Justice of the Province of Quebec, upon an indictment containing two charges, the one for a burglary and felony in breaking and entering in Mr. Thomas Walker's house, at Montreal, on the night of the 6th day of December in the year 1764, with an intention to murder the said Thomas Walker; the other for feloniously and of malice aforethought, cutting off the right ear of the said Thomas Walker, with intention thereby to disfigure him, against the form of the Statute 22 and 23 Car. II, Cap. I, in that case made and provided. Quebec, printed by Brown & Gilmour, 1767." It consists of 46 pages. Mr. Francis Masères prosecuted on part of the Crown as Attorney-General. Mr. Morrison, Mr. Gregory and Mr. Antell were counsel for the prisoner. The prisoner was found not guilty by the Jury, "after withdrawing for about half an hour." The opening address and reply of Masères are given in full.

According to Nova Scotian writers, printing was introduced in Halifax, seven years after its foundation by Cornwallis, 1749. Isaac Curry established a printing press in 1756. The first Nova Scotian newspaper was the *Nova Scotia Chronicle or Weekly Gazette*, published January, 1769, by Anthony Henry, edited by Captain Buckley. Henry subsequently became Queen's Printer, the first appointment of the kind in British America as it is now constituted. He died only in 1800.

of poetry by Lewis Luke Macculloh, Esq. : published by James Lane in Montreal, and to be had of the proprietor by Samuel H. Wilcocke in Burlington, Vermont in 1822." The writer can find no other trace of Macculloh. It appears, however, not unusual at that date to have pamphlets published in Burlington. The writer is in possession of a short treatise on the "Metrical Systems of Horace, arranged on a new and simplified plan by the Rev. F. J. Lundy, S.C.L., Late Scholar of University College, Oxford, and Head-master of the Quebec Classical School, published at Burlington, Vt., by Chauncey Goodrich, 1838."

Le Spectateur Canadien was a weekly paper published in Montreal by C. B. Pasteur & Co. No. 1 appeared 1st June, 1813—the last number 3rd February, 1821. James Lane, publisher ; M. Bibaud, editor. Lane was the publisher of the Scribbler. Could Lewis L. Macculloh be a nom de plume of the versatile elder Bibaud !

L'Aurore weekly appeared in Montreal in October, 1816, the last number, 12th September, 1818.

The first Medical journal was published in Quebec in the latter half of the year 1835, Journal de Medecin de Quebec. The first editor was Doctor Xavier Tessier.

La Bibliothéque Canadienne, published monthly, extends to nine volumes, from June, 1825, to 15th June, 1830. It bears the honoured name of Michel Bibaud. It was followed by L'Observateur ci devant La Bibliothéque Canadienne. The first number appeared 10th July, 1830, the last 2nd July, 1831.

Le Magasin du Bas Canada Journal Litteraire et Scientifique consists of two volumes : January to December, 1832.

L'Encyclopedie Canadienne Journal Litteraire et Scientifique commenced March, 1842, and closed February, 1843.

The Vol. I. seen by the writer bears the additional note of Mr. Jacques Viger "*et unique.*"

The *Canadian Magazine and Literary Repository, Montreal*, printed by N. Mower, was published in 1823 from July to December; six numbers.

The *Canadian Review and Literary and Historical Journal* consists of four volumes, and extends from July, 1824, until February, 1826,

These volumes contain much of the political history of Canada.

Previous to turning to those names which stand out from the writers of that date reference may be made to the early histories of Canada. The first historical treatise is the memorial of Boucher to Colbert in advocacy of the necessity of retaining Canada by France, after its conquest by Kirke. It appeared in 1661. *Histoire véritable et naturelle des mœurs et productions de la nouvelle France vulgairement dit le Canada.* This treatise was translated by the late Mr. Montizambert, of the Senate, one of the descendants of Boucher. It has been published for private circulation *In Memoriam* of the translator; a man held in all respects of life in the highest estimation.

The celebrated *Relations des Jésuites* extend from 1632 to 1672. They were published at various dates in Rouen and Paris, the last appearing in 1673. Subsequent additions, 1672 to 1679, which remained in MS. have been published by Mr. Shea, of New York. The father of our early history is Charlevoix, and he has been followed implicitly by most writers. Charlevoix wrote with the advantage of knowing Canada well, and he had access to many documents which, with his own observations, enabled him to judge events with discrimination. He was a man of genius, power and keen penetration, and as a practised writer his history must ever occupy a distinguished place in our annals. It has been the coil around which all subsequent writers have entwined their narrative.

Of the early days of Canada, up to 1629, we have Champlain's own remarkable productions, together with the works of Sagard, 1636, who was present at the surrender of Quebec to Kirke. L'Escarbot narrates what he gathered together from other sources, for out of Port Royal he is no direct authority. There is no responsible historical writer until 1691, Christien Le Clerq, whose "Etablissement de la Foi" was published at that date. There is a story that this work was suppressed by the Jesuits, and that only a few copies remain : some six or seven are named. The work is undoubtedly scarce, but there is nothing in its pages to support this assertion for the destruction of this volume could not do away with the fact that the Recollets came to the country in 1615, the Jesuits in 1625. The advent of the latter was not an agreeable event to any one in French Canada, Champlain included. Le Clerq tells us how the Recollets were warned that precedence would be obtained by the new comers, '*erunt novissimi primi*' and that Père Noyrot made "*toutes les promisses de reconnaissance et union.*"

This history carries us up to 1675, when Bishop Laval came to Canada, with Duchesneau as Intendent. It gives also the discoveries of La Salle, of the mouth of the Mississippi, and his death in 1687. It closes with an account of the repulse of Phipps before Quebec, 1690. It is dedicated to Frontenac, the best known of French Governors, who died in Quebec, 1698, 28th December, and whose bones lie in the Church of the Recollets. His heart, he directed should be sent back to France, which, it is said, his wife refused to receive, with the remark that as she did not possess it living, she could not accept it lifeless. So it was returned to Canada.

The well-known history of Charlevoix appeared in 1744, and consists of three volumes.

The History of Canada by M. L'Abbe Belmont, Superior of the Seminary, Montreal, between 1713-1724, was published, for the first time, among the historical documents of the Historical Society of Quebec. It is mentioned by Charlevoix. Commencing at the foundation of Quebec in 1603, it is continued till the peace made by M. de Callières in 1699. It may be said to close with the death of Frontenac. It is a work without the least pretension, consisting of only thirty-six pages, and is little more than a mere series of paragraphic memoranda, probably written as an *aide-mémoire* for himself and the ecclesiastics of the Seminary.

Mention must be made of the missing volume of the Memoirs of Bishop Laval. The work is known to have consisted of two volumes. It was written by the Abbé Latour, sometime Vicar-General of Quebec. M. Latour is also known to have corrected the MS. of the *Histoire de l'Hotel Dieu de Quebec*, published at Montauban in 1751. The avowed author of the latter is the Sœur Juchereau de St. Ignace.

The first volume of the Life of Bishop Laval was published nominally at Cologne, 1761. The second volume known to be written has never appeared. The question has often been asked, Has the book been deliberately suppressed ? If so, who were interested in the suppression ? It has been said that the family of the second Bishop St. Vallier were opposed to the publication.

The first history after the Conquest is that of Herriott. " The History of Canada from its first discovery, comprehending an account of the original establishment of the Colony of Louisiana by George Herriott, Esq., Deputy Postmaster-General of British America, Vol. I. London, 1804."

Book I to VIII takes up the narrative to the death of M. de Vaudreuil.

Book IX to XI is devoted to Louisiana proper.

Little need be said of it beyond this description to show its character.

It was followed by the

"History of Canada from its first discovery to the year 1791. By William Smith, Esq., Clerk of Parliament, and Master in Chancery of the Province of Lower Canada. John Neilson, Quebec, 1815." This history, so far as the first volume is concerned, was of use to those who were unable to read the French of Charlevoix. It contains, however, few new facts, how much soever the colouring of them may have been varied. The second volume dwelt on the events following the Conquest, and by linking them together tended to the preservation of their record. It is to Mr. Smith we owe the account of the Walker affair, and to the extraordinary mutiny at Quebec in 1763; and at that day its production had doubtless no little influence on historical research. Its appearance, moreover, was of value in drawing attention to the early history of the country at a period when the struggle for existence of Great Britain in the Continental wars of the first years of the century, with the colossal genius of Napoleon made every fact subordinate to the thought arising from that struggle. The book, however, must be regarded rather as a monument of past than of present service.*

---

*There is a tradition in the family with which the writer is connected by marriage that Mr. Smith borrowed an important MS. from Mr. Lindsay, then Collector of Customs at the Port of St. John's on the Richelieu, on the History of Canada, which, from having been lost or mislaid was never returned.

There is another history of Canada, by Mr. Perrault, exceedingly unpretending, but of merit, and at this date, but indifferently remembered. It was published at intervals. Its title describes its character, *Abrégé de l'histoire du Canada, Première Partie. Depuis sa découverte jusqu' à sa conquête par les Anglais en 1759 et 1760. Redigé par Joseph F. Perrault, Pronotaire, à l'usage des Ecoles Elémentaires.* Québec, 1831.

The second part was published in 1830 [*sic*]. From the establishment of a Legislative Assembly until 1815.

Part three and four appeared in 1833. From the departure of General Prevost, to that of Lord Dalhousie.

Part five in 1836. From the departure of Lord Dalhousie to the arrival of Lord Gosford and the Royal Commission. When nearly eighty, Mr. Perrault published his Autobiography—" written without glasses "—at the request of Lord Aylmer, to whom it is dedicated. Mr. Perrault's name frequently is met in the political literature of this date, and mention of him conveys the idea of his being in all respects an honourable and estimable man.

Mr. Bibaud's history appeared at various intervals. The first volume in 1837. *Histoire du Canada sous la domination Francaise.* The second volume in 1844. *Histoire du Canada et des Canadiens sous la domination Anglaise.* The third volume, edited by his son, Dr. Bibaud, in 1878. It includes the administration of Lord Aylmer and Lord Gosford.

Mr. Bibaud's name, with that of his friend, Mr. Jacques Viger, must always occupy the highest place in Canadian literature; and with all his multifarious writings, it is on the second volume of his history that his fame will chiefly rest. It is, as its title sets forth, a history of Canada and the Canadians, and we know many facts which he has chronicled which otherwise might have passed into oblivion; and he is careful to include incidental notices of the progress of the country, and much which bears upon the habits and tone of thought of that period. Writing of the events which sprung from the disputes concerning the vote on the revenue from 1818 to 1835, he records these events with judgment, temper and moderation. The motto he applied to his history showed that he did not hold the French-Canadian party as a perfectly blameless band of patriots, " Iliacos *intra* muros peccatur et *extra*. The italics are the writers. From the judicial tone of Mr. Bibaud's mind, his memory is not popular with French-Canadian writers. But his honourable and useful life furnishes an example, worthy of imitation, to men both of English and French descent. Mr. Bibaud was born in 1782. He died in 1857. He lived in a time when it was thought something to have the education of a gentleman, and he attained to the position of a good scholar. He was early cast into literary pursuits, and he followed them to the very last days of his life. His industry was remarkable. He literally died in harness, for at the age of seventy-five, he was engaged to translate into French Sir William Logan's Geological Reports, a work which could only be performed by one knowing the subject on which he was writing. Mr. Bibaud published a volume of poems, and it is really difficult to say on what subject of the day he did not touch. He was one of the first who desired that French should be written in purity in Canada,* and not be a *barguinage* of imported

---

*En conséquence de l'ignorance ou de la négligence de nos premiers traducteurs, nos livres de statuts, nos journaux parlementaires et nos autres documents officiels sont farcis de termes qui ne sont rien moins que français là où ils se trouvent. Au lieu de chercher dans un bon dictionnaire la signification des mots anglais qu'ils avaient sous les yeux ces nonchalants traducteurs se sont laissé guider par la simple ressemblance du son ou de l'orthographe. Chez eux *Retour* (traduction littérale de *return*) signifie rapport officiel; *Rappeler* (de to *repeal*) révoquer,

D

phrases, and he endeavoured so to mould his own style. Mr. Bibaud's account of the Government of Lord Dalhousie, extending from 1820 to 1828, may be ranked among the most valuable of his contributions to history.*

Mr. Christie's history is the only additional work to be mentioned within this date.

The first volume was published in 1848; the sixth and last in 1855. It may however with propriety be included within the limits of the period of the histories alluded to, marked by the character and the tone of the political ethics which then prevailed. It is little more than the narrative of events, interspersed with documents of importance. The last

---

abroger, annuler; *Appointer* (de *to appoint*) nommer à un emploi; *Démettre* (de *to desmiss*) destituer; *Instance* exemple, occasion, etc., vol. II, p. 215. M. Bibaud, on one occasion, certainly erred in the opposite direction, " déjà plusieurs belles barques à vapeur vaguaient sur le Saint Laurent entre Québec et Montréal :" (sic) des *pyroscopes* de moindres dimensions sillonnaient les eaux, etc., p. 217. Mr. Bibaud evidently disliked the term bateau à vapeur. So he turned to the Greek *pur* (fire) *skaphis* (a skiff) for a word he could introduce. He gives a paragraph shewing the style of that date, "M. Lee et M. Blanchet ont été *pour* la liste civile et ont été *pour* les mesures *pour* la défense de la province et ont été *pour* qu'il fût prit des mesures *pour* l'éducation," etc., p. 208.

* We are indebted to him that the following is placed on record.

La haine que certains journalistes nourrissaient et paraissaient vouloir inspirer contre Lord Dalhousie, leur faisait accueillir comme plaisanteries de bon goût et du bon ton, des quolibets ou calembourgs que sous une impression différente, ils n'auraient pas crus recevables.

En voyant ce matin (12 Novembre) la cérémonie qui a eu lieu à l'occasion du monument que l'on élève à Wolfe et Montcalm, j'ai songé comme suit; si par une figure de rhétorique Wolfe et Montcalm revenaient en ce monde ne diraient-ils pas; "Hélas ! *vanité* des *vanités*, nous espérions une place parmi les héros, et l'on fait de nous en Canada des admirateurs de patates, des planteurs de choux et des gardes-légumes dans le potager du gouverneur :"

" Jadis dans les combats balançant le destin,
  Voilà Wolfe et Montcalm priapes d'un jardin.
    A moi la médaille offerte."   Vol. II, p. 357.

volume, indeed the most valuable of the collection, consists entirely of public documents, which extend from the time of Mr. Masères to 1855. They principally relate to the times of Sir James Craig and Lord Dalhousie. The history is of value from the information it gives with regard to the earlier legislation, and the many notes appertaining to passing events, and frequent minor statistical notices. It also contains much general information. Mr. Christie leaves the impress of his perfect truth and honesty of purpose.

Prominent in the list of writers after the Conquest, is Francis Masères, for some time Attorney-General of Quebec. He was of a Huguenot family, and lived to the advanced age of ninety-three, dying on the 19th May, 1824. A Cambridge man, he was a mathematician of research and ability. In Canada, he is known by his political writings, especially by the "Freeholder." No one who pretends to write the history of Canada can ignore the evidence of much which he records as passing in the Canada of his day. There is a remarkable essay on the *noblesse* of Canada. His theory was that the French language should in no way be encouraged, and that French institutions should be gradually moulded to the spirit of the British constitution. Any discussion regarding these opinions is out of place in this essay. His works extend over seven volumes. They were published between 1772–79.

Among the archæologists of a later date, Dr. Fisher deserves marked mention. He was a man of unusual attainments, and as the author of the well-known epitaph on Wolfe and Montcalm* will not soon be forgotten. He was a

---

*Although often published it is repeated here :

WOLFE.   MONTCALM.
MORTEM VIRTUS COMMUNEM
FAMAM HISTORIA
MONUMENTUM POSTERITAS
DEDIT
A.D. 1827.

scholar of undoubted merit, a writer of force and power, and of most fascinating manners. He was one of the principal instruments by which the Quebec Literary and Historical Society obtained its high reputation. He came to Canada in 1831, at the instigation of Lord Dalhousie, to edit the *Gazette*. He died at sea in 1849, when returning from England.

But among the archæologists of Quebec, one name especially arises, that of Mr. Jacques Viger. If not the father of Canadian Archæology, his memory will remain in marked prominence in the list. There was a knot of men at that date who peculiarly made the subject a study. Mr. Bibaud has been mentioned; beside him was to be found his friend and *collaborateur* Mr. Viger, but with this distinction that Mr. Viger was a born collector and antiquarian, Mr. Bibaud a man of letters.

Of the same character were Mr. Dennis B. Viger, who moreover played a distinguished part in political life, and whose career was without a blemish or a taint—*si sic semper*. His contributions to literature are not signed, and have no distinguishing mark; Mr. Dominique Mondelet, whose contributions to the Bibliothèque Canadienne are marked by the initials *E. T.*; Dr. Jacques Labrie who signed himself *L.*; Mr. Louis Plamondon, known under the letters *S. H.*; Mr. Jacques Viger signed himself *S. R.* These gentlemen have left many valuable contributions to the political history of the time. One name, however, must be ranged side by side with that of Mr. Viger, that of Mr. J. B. Faribault. Mr. Faribault was Deputy Clerk of the House of Commons, and was an active member of the Historical Society of Quebec. Most of the introductions to the historical publications of the Society were written by him, and the majority of the notes were from his pen. In 1837, he published his Catalogue of Works on the History of America, particularly with regard to that of Canada, Louisiana and Acadia, with biographical, critical and literary notes. The work is difficult to be obtained. A reprint, with additions up to date, would be of the highest value. Why cannot such a work be produced by competent parties? Mr. de Celles, of the Parliamentary Library, is perfectly capable of undertaking this duty.

No student of the History of Canada but must own his deep obligations to the labours of Mr. Faribault.

If mention can be made of Mr. Jacques Viger, it is owing to the great kindness and liberality of the writer's accomplished and learned friend the Abbé Vérrault, one of the first of Canadian Archæologists. It is not an exaggeration to state, that nowhere can such a collection of MSS. and books bearing upon the History of Canada be found, as in his library. There are, doubtless, more extensive collections of books on "America." But this collection of this northern portion of the History of the Continent is simply *unique*. And these books—with rare old editions—blended with modern works up to date, with fine binding, the MS. assorted, the pamphlets* bound are ranged systematically on

---

* Those who are collecting pamphlets may not disdain to be told that the modern mode of binding is to bind them with the paper cover bearing the title. The second blank cover is not included. The possession of this cover commercially adds to the value. A friend of the writer seeing a rare English pamphlet advertised for in the "Bookseller," and possessing it, offered his copy for sale, for it was without his special collection. He received the reply that if it possessed the cover it would fetch three times the amount it would otherwise do. It was without the cover, so he received only sixty shillings instead of a much larger sum. In old days binding was a fine art. The works of Grolier in France, of Roger Paine in England, yet fetch high prices at auctions as binding. In Canada it has not kept pace with other arts, and in our Exhibitions more attention should be given to the subject,

shelves, indexed and catalogued. What a record of patient labour does this work present. Any inquiry for a book is followed immediately by its presence, so admirably and systematically the whole is arranged.

The Abbé Vérrault was good enough to extend to the writer a most cordial and kindly welcome, to receive him for some days as a guest in the institution over which he so devotedly and worthily presides, and without stint or restraint to admit reference to these books and MS., and especially to those of Mr. Jacques Viger. The courtly yet simple grace of Mr. Vérrault's manners, his readiness to impart information, the extent of his reading, his sound learning, his natural acuteness sharpened by travel and intercourse with all kinds of men, made these few days a pleasurable incident in the writer's mind not easily to be forgotten. By these means he is enabled to speak more fully of Mr. Viger. Some literary friends of the writer have thought that the opportunity should not be allowed to pass without special mention of him, that an essay of this character would be incomplete without allusion to Mr. Viger's labours. And these results must not be judged by the standard of what we know to-day.

---

especially in the matter of ordinary binding, for even to-day very fine binding can be produced at a very high price. The binder is an artist in many respects. Certainly in keeping a series of books of the same size and not cutting them down unequally. We have fortunately in Ottawa a very worthy representative of the art in its best days, Mr. Ruthven, of Messrs. Hope & Co.'s establishment, who observes all the minutiæ with the greatest care and attention, while his work is unexceptionable. It is believed that the earliest ancient binding known is that of a copy of "Sancti Hieronyni Epistolæ;" the words stamped at the extremity of the binding towards the edge of the squares are
    Illigatus est Anno Domini, 1469.
     Per me Johannem.
     Richenbach Capellanum,
      In Gyslingen.

What is now to be found in the text even of an elementary work was in the early days of Mr. Viger's labours, without the pale of general attainment. It may perhaps be said that he left few contributions to literature worthy the name. No few of Mr. Viger's labours in this direction were made in connection with Mr. Bibaud. His pseudonym *S. R.* is frequently met in the *Bibliothèque Canadienne*, and all he has written is marked by sense and vigour. He made no pretensions to produce long historical reviews. Nevertheless there remains among his MSS. the mark of long continuous historical labour, especially that portion which dealt with the *status*, personal character and private history of the Roman Catholic clergy. He was also one of the first Editors of the *Quebec Canadien*. Many of the papers preserved by him have been published since his death, and much which is given to the world was owing to the fact that the documents had been preserved by him. Thus in the *Invasion de Canada* by the Abbé Vérrault, 1873, that writer remarks: " Almost all the remaining memoirs were collected by the Commander Viger, who, thirty years ago, entertained the idea of publishing all that he could bring together on *la guerre des Bostonnais*, as it is yet called in our country parishes. . . . It was at the close of the war of 1812, in which he served with honour, that Mr. Viger formed the project of commencing this publication. . . . It is to the Commander Viger that the principal merit of this publication is due." The Abbé further tells us that, doubtless, there is much personal information which Mr. Viger had obtained which he failed to write down.

The Jesuits' Journal is another case in point. It was published by Mr. Desbarats, but most of the edition was destroyed at the fire of his premises in Ottawa. The book is therefore rare. Its early history is curious. Mr. Cochrane,

Private Secretary to Sir John Cope Sherbrooke, then Governor-General, found the MSS., with some waste paper, carelessly placed at the bottom of a cupboard, evidently designed to furnish matter to light the stove. Mr. Cochrane saved it from destruction. Mr. Viger carefully copied it and preserved it. In his day it was indeed a rarity.

Mr. Viger, a man of good family, started life with an excellent education, and he is one of those men, who in their career, furnish an answer to the query, What is the use of learning Latin? The influence on him was to make him careful, exact, painstaking, conscientious and methodical, moreover to show by his labours that he held perfect correctness to be indispensable to all he did, and that truth was the first duty of life. His MSS. are deliberately written in a clear hand, and nearly every copy is attested that it had been collated with the original. He was born in 1787. The war of 1812 broke out, and in common with the leading French-Canadian gentry, he joined the forces raised in the Province to withstand the invasion from the United States. He rose to be a Commander in the Voltigeurs, and among other affairs, was present on the 27th May, 1813, on the attack on Sackett's Harbour, marred at the moment of success by the wretched indecision of the incompetent Prevost. The war over, he turned to civil life, and was engaged in Montreal to some extent in his profession as a Surveyor. He was the first Mayor of Montreal, in 1832, and throughout his life held high position in the community. He married the widow of Captain Lennox, a near connection of the Duke of Richmond, and was long known as one of the most distinguished members of Montreal society. A miniature of him being in the study of the Abbé Vérrault, it would be a graceful act for the Corporation of Montreal to hang in their Council

Chamber a portrait of their first Mayor,* especially one so renowned in Canadian history.

The MSS. left by Mr. Viger, now in Mr. Vérrault's possession, extend over several volumes. Mr. Viger has twenty-nine volumes, which he calls "*ma saberdache*." No one can suppose an old Voltigeur like Mr. Viger, who had long carried his *sabertache* attached to his sabre could be ignorant how to spell the word. For as he uses it, it is neither French nor English.† Not to speak of the marks of his

---

*Speaking of the Portraits of Mayors in Montreal; after Mr. McGill's retirement from the position in 1843, his friends subscribed for a testimonial, which took the form of a portrait, for his services as Mayor. Mr. Charles Wilson was equally honoured. His portrait also hung in the Civic Council Chamber. Some days after the Gavazzi riots in 1851, during which it was urged against Mr. Wilson that it was he who gave the command to fire,— a command so disastrously obeyed by the troops who had been called out—Mr. Sexton, then City Clerk, informed the writer, that some United States ladies of distinction were brought by a prominent citizen to view the City Hall. Mr. Sexton accompanied them. A curtain always being drawn for protection before these two portraits, which were the size of life, Mr. Sexton acting as *cicerone* drew back the curtain of the Wilson portrait. He started back aghast. The frame contained a blank. The astonishment of all present was extreme, for such a step had never in any way been anticipated. A close investigation was made to discover the perpetrator of the Vandalism. Every engine of inquiry was set on foot, but those who executed it remained undiscovered. Shortly after, the portrait of the late Mr. McGill shared the same fate. The latter certainly was the work of a small knot of men, and was merely an expression of the *lax talionis* for the universal respect in which Mr. McGill was held, was a guarantee that he was without an enemy. It is lamentable that political passion should condescend to these contemptible proceedings, for which the following generation can only blush for shame.

†The *sabretache* is a small portable pocket of about nine inches by four, attached by straps to the sword belt to hang *dégagé* by the sabre. In the Cavalry it is a mark of rank, and is used from the Colonel to the Corporal. It can contain papers, states, the roster. On service, it is often made to hold a tallow candle for wet boots, a knife and fork, pipe and tobacco, a corkscrew, a pocket handkerchief, and other luxuries of the kind on a campaign.

education, and his knowledge of both French and English, the title itself is suggestive of some pleasantry, and the orthography he uses is additional proof of some hidden meaning. Whatever it might have been it is lost. No explanation has been found of it. These volumes contain many documents yet unpublished bearing upon Canadian history. As has been remarked some of the collection has been made known. Many of them bear on the early years of the eighteenth century, when the struggle for rule on the continent between France and England was being fought out : also much bearing on the second half century, especially the writings of Mr. Masères. The series contains some few portraits and sketches of old forts, with some water-colour drawings by Duncan, a Montreal artist of great merit, of a quarter of a century back. Among other sketches, there is one of the celebrated Fort Duquesne on the Ohio, evidently a contemporary production, showing where Braddock was defeated. There is very much in these volumes which canced. There is very much in these volumes which can be advantageously printed.

There are also 5 volumes of Opuscules of matters edited by Mr. Viger, with original contributions.

3 volumes of the Journal de Missions 1811-1816.
3   "   "   Annals of the Hotel Dieu, Montreal.
13   "   of Private Letters.
4   "   of the Clergy of Canada, with MS. corrections
         of the name, place of birth, and career,
with several folio volumes, containing much information of the events since the Conquest. One of these gives in full detail the proceedings of the Committee to which Mr. Viger was Secretary, to concert means to prevent the passage of the bill in the Imperial Parliament in 1822 to form a Union of the Canadas known as the "Canadian Trade Act." A serious misunderstanding arose relative to the import duties

collected in Lower Canada, Upper Canada claiming a larger amount than it was receiving, with corresponding arrearages. The first impulse of Lower Canada was to refuse to recognize the right of Upper Canada in any form, as the resolutions of the 16th of February, 1822, clearly establish. Moreover, the difficulties which had arisen since 1818, as to the mode of voting supplies, had even become more complicated. The Imperial Parliament brought in this bill, which regulated the relations of the two Provinces by forming them into one body. It was strongly opposed by the French Canadian party in Lower Canada, and in Upper Canada received but little countenance, the dominant party desiring to see no change in the political government of the Province. The records of the proceedings in Montreal, as presented by Mr. Viger, are to be found in this volume.

One curious MS. volume is known as the *Chambre de Justice de Longueuil, 1761 to 1764*. After the conquest, before the organization of the new Law Courts, all civil points of difference were referred for decision to officers of militia. It was considered that those holding these positions were men of character and intelligence and acquainted with the old laws of the country, and that under such circumstances substantial justice would be given in disputes between the "new" subjects. This volume is a record of the litigation during these years in the Court of Longueuil, no few being signed by Toussaint Trudeau, the ancestor of Mr. Toussaint Trudeau, the Deputy Minister of Railways and Canals.

It is not possible to enter at any length into the contents of these many volumes. It is anticipated that, as occasion offers, much of their contents will be given to the world. It is evident that it can only be produced advantageously by care being taken that the portions hitherto published are not reproduced and unnecessary expense incurred. Moreover it is indispensable that what is published be complete and above criticism.

It is the non-observance of this principle which has led to some unpleasantness with regard to the appearance of the *Collection de Manuscrits contenant lettres, Mémoires et autres documents Historiques relatifs à la nouvelle France*, lately published by the Quebec Government. These papers extend from 1650 to the conquest, with some additional matter carried on to 1789. With all the criticism urged against the volumes, the Quebec Government, and especially Mr. Blanchet, who took a prominent part in the production, deserve the thanks of every man of letters. When the **first** volumes appeared some strange misconception arose concerning them. It was evident that a great many passages had **been** erased, and it was stated that the mutilation had been made at Quebec. This question has been set fully at rest by a letter from Mr. Parkman, the distinguished historian, addressed to Mr. Blanchet. It appears that the documents in Boston, from which the Quebec printed books were taken, were copied in France in 1846 by Mr. Perley Poore, who was employed "to make a collection of French documents bearing directly or indirectly on the early history of that part of the country." What omissions are to be found are due to Mr. Poore, who seems to have considered his labours to be limited to transcribe what appertained to his own State. Before these documents were printed they had the reputation of being of more value than they really are. It has since been discovered that many of them were previously well known, and the incomplete condition in which many appear detracts greatly from the value of the whole. The mistake was, in not going direct to Paris and seeking the originals instead of taking copies from imperfect transcripts. But with all this, it is to be said that Mr. Blanchet is **entitled to** the public thanks for his zeal in Archæology. *Experientia docet*.

There can be no doubt of the value **of** the next publications promised, *Les Jugements* **de** *delibérations du Conseil Souverain de Quebec*. It is looked for by Archæologists with great interest.

This announcement **has also led** to the inquiry—where are the *Registres de l'Ancien Conseil* which existed before 1663, the date at which the *Conseil Supérieur* was established. **The value** of these papers will be everywhere conceded, **and they** should be preserved. The Dominion Government **should** take steps to obtain possession **of them, wherever they may** be, and some responsible person should **be delegated to seek** for them. They are the property of **no private corporation** or individuals. They do not appertain, **even to any Province.** That they exist is suggested by the fact that both **Abbé** Ferland and Abbé Faillon allude to them as authority in special notes. They are the property of the Dominion. While writing on this subject it may be well to mention the reports which **are current as to** the *Registres Civils de la Prévoté de Quebec*. **It is to the** effect that, in **place** of being put in the **hands of** competent **men,** who **can do** justice **to the work,** which requires **special** aptitude and **care,** they **are given** out at the request of members of **the** Legislative Assembly to such of their constituents **who need** employment. The writer knows nothing **of** the facts. It will greatly relieve the public mind if it be authoritatively announced that such **is not** the case ; that the originals are **not sent away** from Quebec ; **that** they are rigorously kept **safely ; and** that no risk **is** incurred by transferring them **to a country parish,** here **and** there, **as the means of** gratifying **some bustling** member. The **work is important, and should be given to** experienced persons, while the original documents should be jealously guarded.

The publication of these *Registres* will be valueless unless it be carried out systematically and carefully. What use will they be to anyone without a perfectly arranged analytical index? The text should be likewise accompanied by notes of a learned and able commentator. If this book be issued to the world, without this careful and necessary editing, the publication will be simply a waste of public money. Equally will it prove a literary crime to confer a most unenviable reputation on its perpretator. The proofs should at once be placed in the hands of competent persons to perform this duty. "Laval" can furnish, it safely may be assumed, many gifted men to perform it. The example so honourably set by the late Abbé Laverdière in his edition of Champlain is a proof what can be done.

There is one distinguished French Canadian, whose fame in political life and on the Bench would in no way lead to the belief that his name can claim a marked place in this essay: the illustrious Sir Hypolite Lafontaine. But the fact is that he has left much behind him denoting his devotion to Archæology. In order to give his judgment on the Seigneurial Tenure question, it is no exaggeration to say that he studied every document he could possibly lay his hands on. The fact is denoted by the many MS. books which he left behind him in which these documents are copied in his own hand, and the other volumes he hired scribes to write for him. He had an excellent library himself, containing all the books bearing on Canada which he could collect, and he possessed the only known complete set of the fyles of the *Quebec Gazette* from its first number. The MSS. volumes he left behind him are of great value. His celebrated judgment on the Seigneurial Tenure yet exists in MS. in the possession of the Abbé Vérrault. It consists of ten books, foolscap size, each containing 100 pages. It is written in a clear, legible clerk-like hand, with scarcely an erasure, in Sir Hypolite's caligraphy, from beginning to end. He also left behind him 34 thick volumes of valuable pamphlets collected by him, about 400 in number.

A notice of the Archæology of Quebec would be wanting in completeness if allusion were not made to the admirable edition of Champlain's works, brought out under the protection of Laval University, by the late Abbé C. N. Laverdière. The work is not simply an honour to the University under the auspices of which it appeared, but it reflects credit on the whole Dominion. The typography, the paper, the *fac simile* of the original engravings and maps, the excellent character of the notes, evincing both honesty and research, the thorough truth and genuineness with which the narrative is given, all these make the work itself in every way remarkable. It was published in 1870, entirely without the date to which the remarks on this branch of Canadian history are directed. But this edition of Champlain is a matter entirely of itself, and, dealing with the first chapters of our annals, exacts mention, not only from the subject, but from the admirable manner in which the lamented editor fulfilled his labours. His reward will be that his name will always take a first place in Canadian literature.

The remarkable labours of the Abbé Tanguay equally merit acknowledgment, although he is still engaged on his *Dictionnaire Genéalogique des Familles Canadiennes*. For the last twenty-five years he has been occupied in tracing from the Church registers the family history of French-Canadian descent, with the various foreign elements which have been engrafted upon it. The fact is that to speak of the French-Canadian race as a pure and direct offspring of France in every respect is scarcely possible. The majority in the Province, numerically, from the earliest days of the present political rule, on all occasions, and as a consequence, without hindrance or delay, they have absorbed all the foreign elements which, by marriage, became connected with them. The race to-day is, therefore, as composite to some extent as the old Saxon race of England, which, with its union with Danes, Northmen and Normans, formed the present English race. The accessions to the French stock since the Conquest of these outer relationships cannot have failed to have communicated their impress of lineage. English, Irish, Scotch, Germans, have all, in one or two generations, become a part of the present French Canadian population, as many a family name plainly testifies, to what extent remains yet to be determined. The Abbé Tanguay is a case in point. He is of German descent, and, it is claimed, that this persevering, unswerving, untiring pursuit of his system is an inherited gift of his Teutonic blood.

His peculiar task has been to seek in the Parochial registers, Notarial acts, and other family papers, all this genealogical information, which he has embodied in a dictionary, so that the whole family connections of French rule during the century of its activity—indeed, from the early days of Champlain—can be distinctly made known.

The dictionary includes about a century of this information. The volumes about to appear will contain sixty years additional. A production, in every way remarkable, without parallel, and marked by conscientious correctness. M. l'Abbé Tanguay is equally an accomplished scholar and a zealous, sound archæologist. His numerous friends look forward to many years continuance of his useful labours.

The registration which has existed in the parishes of Lower Canada almost from the very first day of their foundation may be safely said to be without parallel in the world. These *Registres de l'état civil*, as they are called, present a curious and positive family record of French Canadian Roman Catholic family life. The outline of each family relationship is there distinctly to be traced. That it is authentic is indisputable. Thus the unbroken chain of historical pedigree runs back from the present hour to the first days of New France, in the seventeenth century. Identification of a family is simple in the extreme, for the birth of a child is affiliated not simply to the father, but equally to the mother under her maiden name, with the place whence she came. It is the remarkable industry and power of organization to systematize and place this information side by side to make it easy of reference, and to apply it to every day life, which is the distinguishing feature of the Abbé Tanguay's labour. There is not a Roman Catholic family in the Province of Quebec, however humble, which cannot trace its lineage to its first known progenitors in the Dominion.

It seems strange to us to believe that scarcely a half-century has passed since steps were taken in England and Wales to obtain correct registration of births, marriages and deaths. It was only in 1836 that the better method was introduced by the Act 6 and 7, Will. IV., c. 80. A uniform mode of proceeding was then established, when much the same system was followed which had prevailed for upwards of two centuries previously in Canada. At this date the surname of the mother is equally exacted with that of the father and all the accessory facts bearing upon the child's birth. Until that date registration had been left with the Rectors and Vicars of parishes. By some conscientious men it was carefully and attentively watched, by others given over

E

to the parish clerks. So every parish register depended on the character of those who formed it, and in few cases was any supervision exercised: and, as has been remarked, scarcely half a century has elapsed since this imperfect and unsatisfactory mode of proceeding in Imperial England has passed away.

Would it be entirely out of place for an inquiry to be made how this duty is being performed outside of the *giron* of the Roman Catholic Church throughout the Dominion? No one can doubt the necessity of care, system and methodical attention. For all recognize the extent to which important interests are involved by this duty being carefully performed, and of admitted correctness. Perhaps the great difficulty in establishing a uniform system throughout the Dominion is that the registration is under Provincial control. In any case the question is a very complicated one.

In no way a part of Canadian Archæology, but having an intimate connection with it, especially with that of the Province of Quebec, is the "official" translation of the term "Dominion." It is rendered by the incorrect, meaningless, so far as this country is concerned, barbarous word "*Puissance*." The term receives recognition from no one educated French-Canadian gentleman of authority in the literary world. It is adhered to only by men of little intelligence and as a mere means of preserving political traditions personally useful to themselves.

The so-called translation originated with the late Sir George Cartier*, who felt a sensitiveness regarding it which led many of his friends to avoid all allusion to the word. The death of Sir George Cartier, now nearly thirteen years back, makes further reticence uncalled for.

The word Dominion was not really applied to Canada for the first time in 1867. As a term it is of long standing on this Continent, having been the title of the State of Virginia early in its history. It has upwards of a century of life in connection with the Dominion as it exists to-day. In an

---

* During the first Parliament after Confederation, a Bill was before the House of Commons in Committee. Mr. Chauveau, the present Sheriff of Montreal, who then represented the County of Quebec, and at the same time was Minister of Public Instruction, and First Minister of his Province, was the Chairman. When the proceedings had reached the last stage of adopting the preamble of the Bill, the late Mr. Holton, member for Chateauguay, rose in his place, and with more than his usual blandness commenced his remarks by congratulating the House, that in view of the question he had to put, one so scholarly and capable as the Chairman occupied the chair. With some just remarks to the well-known attainments and reading of Mr. Chauveau, Mr. Holton proceeded to say that he would call the attention of the Minister of Public Instruction of the Province of Quebec to what he thought a very incorrect translation of the word Dominion. It was rendered by "Puissance," which, in his (Mr. Holton's) opinion, meant entirely the contrary to Dominion, a view in which he was sustained by every educated French Canadian he had spoken to on the subject. He claimed that the House had a right to an expression of opinion from the learned Chairman. Mr. Chauveau looked steadily before him to the speaker: whatever his thoughts, they never found expression, for he had no opportunity for criticism even of the mildest shade. Sir George Cartier jumped up with more than his usual excitability and in a sharp angry tone, at the highest key in which he could speak, may be said to have shrieked : "*Oui, monsieur le Président, c'est Puissance, c'est moi qui ai voulu que ce fut Puissance et tant que j'aurai de la puissance, ce sera Puissance.*"

The House burst into a roar of laughter, and a subdued tone of merriment took the place of debate, during which Mr. Chauveau quietly declared the preamble carried, and evidently to his delight in

address to the people of Great Britain from the "Delegates appointed by the several English Colonies of New York, ... and South Carolina, to consider of their grievances in general Congress, at Philadelphia, September 5, 1774," the following passage occurs :—

And by another Act, "*the Dominion of Canada* is to be so extended, modelled and governed," as that by being disunited from us, detached from our interests by civil as well as religious prejudices, that by their numbers swelling with Catholic emigrants from Europe, and by their devotion to administration so friendly to their religion, they might become formidable to us, and on occasion be fit instruments in the hands of power to reduce the ancient free Protestant Colonies to the same state of slavery with themselves.

It has not been possible to find the document whence the expression "Dominion" is taken. It is not in the Royal proclamation of 7th Oct., 1763 ; nor in the Quebec Act of 13th January, 1774, in which the expression used is the "Territory of Canada ;" nor in the Act " to establish a fund towards further defraying the charges of the administration of justice and support of Civil Government." But wherever the term was then used, it is of ancient date, and in resuming it in 1867, we were only falling back on the designation of the country, before it was done away with by the Acts of 1774 and 1791.

---

escaping an embarrassing question—for whatever Mr. Chauveau's political adherence to Sir George Cartier, there is no reason to suppose that he was prepared to defend his literary efforts in this direction— left the Chair and reported "the Bill as amended." This incident is not only remarkable for an early protest against the translation without a single word being uttered in its defence : but it is believed to be the sole instance when Mr. Holton posed before the House as a *farçeur*. Sir George's amiability of character, and the respect felt for his memory have, alone sustained his view to this day. It is time that the House should act as Mr. Chauveau on that occasion, in the reverse direction, quietly change the word to what it should be. Sir George Cartier's ground for its preservation, calls to mind a sentence of Erasmus's, in his *Encomium, Moriæ* : " *Quis enim me melius exprimat quam ipsa me ?*" It is Moria who speaks.

Any student of language knows the word to be perfectly untranslatable : indeed, in adopting it into French, that there was only one course to be followed : to retain it, giving it a character to adapt it to the genius of the language to which it was transferred. It was Mr. Arthur Buies who suggested the proper course on this occasion ; to change the gender which euphony exacts for words with this termination, which is feminine, and to make it masculine, calling it *Le Dominion*. If ever there was a case where the line of Pope, "the sound should bear an echo to the sense," is well applied, it is here. The consequence is that with educated French-Canadian writers, who are without the domain of political intrigue and party combinations, the word "*puissance*" is treated as if it did not exist. It has entirely lost its associations, and hence its power ; correctness it never possessed. The time has come when French is to be written in our national state papers with purity and elegance ; and one of the first steps in this direction is to do away with the barbarous word *puissance* as a French equivalent of our national designation in the Imperial system of Great Britain.

Bearing upon the subject, it may be remarked that, fortunately, we can refer to a work of unusual merit and of equal geographical correctness lately issued in Paris. The frequenter of Parisian *salons* needs not to be told of the ability, power and reputation of M. Onésime Reclus. Last year his work, *La Terre à vol d'Oiseau* was completed. If anyone is desirous of testing the correctness of the criticism made in these pages let him turn to this book *(passim)* especially page 632, he will there find Canada designated as "*le Dominion.*"

With an authority of this character, will our Parliamentary translators be permitted to continue in their evil ways ?

Two works, which were published in England at the time of the Conquest, and in the years succeeding it, may with propriety be mentioned. The First " The Natural and Civil History of the French Dominions in North and South America, giving a particular account of climate, soil, minerals, animals, vegetables, manufactures, trade, commerce and language; together with the religion, government, genius, character, manners and customs of the Indians and other inhabitants, illustrated by maps and plans of the principal places, collected from the best authorities, and engraved by T. Jefferies, geographer to H. R. H. the Prince of Wales. Part I. A description of Canada and Louisiana. London : Printed for Thomas Jefferies, at Charing Cross, 1760."

The second work is " The History of the British Dominions in North America, from the first discovery of that vast continent by Sebastian Cabot, in 1497, to its present glorious establishment, as confirmed by the late Treaty of Peace in 1763. In fourteen books. London : Printed for W. Strachan, and T. Becket & Co., in the Strand, 1773."

This work is attributed to Oldmixon. Little need be said of it, 26 pages only are devoted to Canada (pp. 194-219). It describes the geography and climate, and gives some account of the Indian population, likewise of the natural history, and products of the country.

Jefferies' is a far more important work. Although published immediately after the taking of Quebec, the book must have been commenced previous to that date. It is not impossible that it may have been suggested by the taking of Louisbourg, in 1758. It gives maps of the operations before that place, and likewise those of Quebec. It contains, also, an account of the geography of Canada, as it was then known, and in a general way records the history of French domination. At the period when it was published it must have been of much value, for it contains many other valuable maps, and is the source of the information which in this respect we possess to-day. The account of the taking of Louisbourg furnishes many details of the siege, and the despatch of Wolfe from Quebec, of the 2nd September, 1759, with those of Monckton and Townshend, and Admiral Saunders are given in full.

What adds to the value of the work is the opinion it expresses of the Canadian population soon to become British subjects. And with its passing allusion to the public sentiment of the then British Colonies to the South, it is evident that thoughtful men already discerned the seeds of the future difficulties, which ended in the disseverance of the relationship. The French Canadian will, however, have the satisfaction of seeing that it was under no depreciatory estimate of his character that he became incorporated into the outer British Empire. The following is the opinion expressed at that date as it is set forth in Jefferies' (p. 9) :—

It is remarked of the *Canadians* that their conversation is enlivened by an air of freedom which is natural and peculiar to them ; that they speak the *French* in the greatest purity, and without the least false accent. There are few rich people in that colony, though they all live well, are extremely generous and hospitable, keep very good tables, and love to dress very finely. They are reckoned well made and to have an exceeding fine complexion, witty in their conversation, polite in their behaviour, and most obliging in their manners. The *Canadians* have carried the love of arms and of glory so natural to their mother country along with them, for which reason they have little of the narrow, selfish spirit of the merchant in them, and as they never entertain any thought of amassing, they have, therefore, little to lose ; so that war is not only welcome to them, but coveted with extreme ardour. It is easy to imagine the consequence of such neighbors to the *British* Colonies, immersed in luxury, and a prey to all the passions which accompany ease and riches, were the Canadians headed by such generals as France formerly had, with an ambitious and wise prince on the throne. Great Britain, therefore, cannot be too watchful and expeditious to prevent the danger, whilst her precautions are of any moment or avail to her.

The literary history of Ontario is so intermingled with the political agitation which took its rise in the years succeeding the war of 1812—to reach its climax in 1836—that, to-day, it is only wise to allude to it with moderation and delicacy. The weapons which were used in those quarrels are still possessed by the sons and grandsons of the chief actors : some of the latter, even, have not reached the prime of life. In instances these arms yet retain their brightness, and, therefore, they can be brought to the contest of to-day with the old bitterness of spirit. Is it the duty of history to revive old feuds with more than old vigour, the narrative of facts remaining the same ?* For they have so often been given to the world that, unless papers are produced which are not now known, there is little which is new to be told. It can be but of slight advantage to refurbish the old narrative. We must bear in mind that in political turmoil the fault seldom lies entirely on one side. The truth is peculiarly apparent in the early years of Upper Canada. The issue at stake was imperfectly understood. The slightest manifestation of a Liberal tendency was regarded as a desire to throw off British allegiance, and hence those who objected to much which was then practised and experienced, sustained the existing Government, while they severely criticised it. The theory also was advanced that monarchical governments were unprogressive, and it was a proof of the doctrine to point out the progress of the State of New York in contradistinction to that of Upper Canada. In judging the conduct of the

---

*As the process of these narratives is now bringing me among my contemporaries, I begin to feel myself "walking upon ashes under which the fire is not extinguished," and coming to the time of which it will be proper rather to say "nothing that is false than all that is true."

Johnson's Lives of the Poets.
ADDISON.

leading men of the Province up to 1830, we ought also to bear in mind, the condition of the Home Government in the reign of George IV. The only avenue by which position could be obtained was through the broad path of extreme Tory opinion; and the leading officials in Canada,—certainly those representing Imperial power—necessarily partook of the views of those who named them. Especially it was the case of the military officers formed in the school of the Duke of Wellington, many of whom could not even apprehend the political requirements of the hour. The difficulty was to know the path to follow, and the solution could only be evolved by time and patience, the latter a virtue which neither party possessed. One fact is undoubted. The high personal character, and sense of honour which distinguished these men. Not one has been accused of intrigue or dereliction of duty. We had to form and shape our Constitution, and it was to be determined by events. So far as this generation can judge, it was not until 1829 that even a glimpse of the solution of the difficulty appears. It was in that year that Mr. Stanley, afterwards the celebrated Lord Derby,* presented a petition to the Imperial Parliament from 3,000 inhabitants, asking for a "local and responsible administration," but it is a question if the machinery by which this result could be gained was distinctly felt and known. And, it must be recollected that this event took place in the Mother Country before the passage of the Reform Bill. The political impulse given by that measure needs no comment.

The early literary efforts of Upper Canada were purely political, and it was only as material advance was made that any development in the higher arts can be looked for. Hence the first years of Western Canada, devoted mainly to

---

*The translator of Homer.

the struggle for existence, can shew little record of high culture. There was, in these days, but little commerce, in contradistinction to trade. The only requirement for the public wants was the ordinary storekeeper. Time had to develop the higher rank of enterprise.

And what progress has been made in Ontario ? As we drive through the busy, active, animated, well-built city of Toronto,* it seems scarcely possible to believe that

---

*On the 6th March, 1834, during the rule of Sir John Colborne, York was incorporated a city under the name of Toronto. Its extent was then increased. According to La Hontan at the close of the seventeenth century, the large bay extending from the mouth of the River Severn, discharging from Lake Simcoe, and reaching Penetanguishene, —the present Matchedash Bay—at that date was known as the Bay of Toronto. In order to reach Lake Ontario from Lake Huron the portages were made up the Severn to Lake Simcoe, then called Lake Toronto [une rivière qui sort du petit lac du même nom] and the waters of the lake followed to what is now known as Holland River, which runs from the South. From this river a portage led to the River Tonaonta—the present Don—and it was at its mouth that Lake Frontenac—Lake Ontario—was gained. This was the route followed from the St. Lawrence to Lake Huron. On Charlevoix's Map of 1745, Lake Simcoe is shown as Lake Taronto.

There cannot be a doubt, Lake Simcoe and its waters discharging into Georgian Bay, were known originally as Lake and River Toronto, and the name appears even to have extended to some of the waters reaching the Bay of Quinte. The French fort, which was to the West of the present site of the city, not far from the Humber, and built by M. de la Jonquière in 1749, was named Fort Rouillé, after the French Colonial Minister.

The application of the name to the present city of Toronto appears in Smyth's Gazetteer, a work published in London, in 1799. He there gives "Toronto Bay, now called York Harbour," and the "Toronto River, now called the Humber." He also speaks of the "Old French Fort" Toronto. In the early French maps, the site of Toronto is marked as Teiaigou—with some difference of orthography. Bouchette calls the published map of his admirable survey, 12th August, 1815—Plan of York Harbour.

I applied to Mr. Brymner, the learned Director of the Archive Branch, for such information as the office could furnish on the subject.

DeRochefoucauld, ninety years back, described the place as a cluster of a few houses round the barracks containing the Simcoe Rangers. And Toronto is something more than a large commercial centre. As a city, in the attributes of what the Romans called urbanity, in its social life, its University, its culture, its incipient cosmopolitanism it rises above Buffalo, Cincinnati, and even Chicago, although it may be inferior to either in wealth and population.

I owe to his labours the ability to state that, in 1788, the name of Toronto was, undoubtedly applied to its present site. The fact is established by the draft instructions to Captain Gother Mann, Royal Engineers (afterwards Major-General), dated Headquarters, Quebec, 29th May, 1788, unsigned, instructing him to examine the mouth of French River, that of the River Matchedash Lake Huron, likewise, *Toronto on Lake Ontario.* Further, by two letters of Major Littlehales, Brigade Major to General Simcoe. Both are dated *York, late Toronto,* the first, 27th August, 1793; the second, 5th September, 1793. Moreover, *Le Petit Atlas Maritime par le S. Bellin, Ingénieur de la Marine,* 1764 (four years after the conquest), shows "Fort Toronto."

Mr. Brymner also writes me "of the fact that the name Toronto was applied to different places, there is proof to be obtained from old maps. Bellin's map of 1755 gives Lake Ontario, but without a single settlement to the North; and it shows *Lac Toronto* to the south east of Lake Huron. Another map, by Janson d'Abbeville, of 1656, gives the same Lake as *Oontaron* and the river called Toronto in Bellin's map of 1755 is called Tarontonanerenon. Taronton being, according to the early map, the name of the head waters of the Rivière des Prairies, falling into the Ottawa near Montreal."

In the documents relating to the Colonial History of New York, published by the New York Legislature, Vol. x, p. 200, under date 30th April, 1749, in an "Abstract of despatches from Canada," we read of "Fort built at Toronto,—on the north-west of Lake Ontario, twenty-five leagues from Niagara, and seventy-five from Fort Frontenac."

It appears then that the district extending from Lake Simcoe southward was originally called Toronto, that the Fort was called Fort Rouillé, and was for some time so recognized by the French Government: that previous to the final struggle the name Toronto was applied to the site of the present city: and that after the conquest, the locality was known by that name again to be given to the City of York, when that city ceased to be so called.

With all its advantages of water communication, and its connection with the Upper Lakes, there was great hesitation whether the future capital of Western Canada should be established on its present site or taken to the River de la Trenche, now called the Thames. Governor Simcoe's idea was to establish a city on the banks of this river, the theory of the present London, although there is nothing to show that this identical position was selected, for all was wilderness. Toronto, itself, was known as the starting point of a trail which ran to Holland Landing, thirty miles from the Lake, which there met the river discharging into Lake Simcoe, and by the egress of the waters of the Lake, connection was made with Lake Huron. It was the route long followed to Lake Superior, a fact which may account for the late settlement of the Counties of Bruce and Grey. Lord Dorchester, then Governor-General, persevered in his view that Kingston, at the end of Lake Ontario, should be the naval station of the Lakes, and it was owing to some want of accord between Lord Dorchester and Governor Simcoe that the latter was recalled. Both were men of noble character and enlarged views, devoted to duty, and with a high sense of patriotism. The great distance between Quebec and Newark—the present Niagara—the time exacted to make the journey, and the difficulty and, perhaps, the expense, in those days of limited expenditure, may have all prevented the meeting. Simcoe came to Canada in 1792. He was a man of fortune and a member of the Imperial Parliament, and there could have been few personal inducements to lead him to accept the position. He remained until 1796. During his day the seat of Government was at Newark, the present Niagara, and the first broadsheet of a newspaper was published there in 1793. The Government offices were removed to Toronto in the administration of the Government by Mr. Peter Russell.

This first newspaper may be regarded to-day as an admirable specimen of typography. It appeared on the 18th April, 1793, under the title of the *Upper Canada Gazette ; or, American Oracle.* Its first printer was Louis Roy. The last number printed at Niagara is Vol. VI., No. 187, dated 25th August, 1798. No. 188 was brought out at York, Thursday, 4th October, 1798.

The *Constellation* took its place in Niagara. It was commenced the 20th July, 1799, and was continued until 18th January, 1800.

The *Niagara Herald* succeeded, and lasted from the 7th January, 1801 (No. 2. is dated Jan. 24), to 28th August 1802.

The Upper Canada Gazette, or American Oracle, removed to York, continued on until 28th March, 1807, when the last number under that title was issued. (Vol. XVI., No. 50.) Vol. XVI., No. 51, came out as the York *Gazette*, 15th April, 1807, John Cameron, editor. Mr. Tiffany ceasing to direct it, Dr. Scadding informs us that, in 1817, Dr. Horne became the editor, and called it the *Upper Canada Gazette*, and that, in 1821 it was divided into the *Upper Canada Gazette* and the *Weekly Gazette*. Mr. Fothergill, becoming the Government printer, named a portion of it *The Weekly Register*. A speech of Mr. Fothergill, in 1825—for he was a member of the House of Assembly—on the Post Office revenue claiming that information concerning it should be laid before the House, led to his removal from the position by the then Governor, Sir Peregrine Maitland ; and that there should be no more mistakes about the politics of the paper—Mr. Fothergill had shewn strong Liberal tendencies in the House —Mr. Stanton, who had been appointed Queen's Printer, called the unofficial portion *The U. E. Loyalist.* Such is the history of the first paper established in Upper Canada to the date named. After his dismissal, Mr. Fothergill started the *Palladium*, 1825. The writer can find no evidence of its duration.

It will with difficulty be believed by those, who to-day contemplate the important and wealthy Province of Ontario, that no printed book out of the domain of Statute Law, and the Parliamentary Journals can be discovered prior to the year 1832[*]: only a few years more than half a century back. The title is "History of the late War between Great Britain and the United States of America, with a retrospective view of the causes from whence it originated, collected from the most authentic sources; to which is added an appendix containing public documents, etc., relating to the subject. By David Thompson, late of the Royal Scots, Niagara, U.C. Printed by T. Sewell, Printer, Bookbinder and Stationer, Market Square, 1832." It must be remembered that the first Ontario newspaper was issued thirty-nine years previously, in 1793. During this period, excepting the years of the war, there was constant political excitement, and as a theory the opinion must suggest itself, that some pamphlet advocating a policy, some defence of personal conduct, must have been given to the world previous to 1832. So far as the writer's inquiry determines, not one publication of the character named has survived as a landmark of the literary power of that date. In 1824 the population in Ontario was but a few souls over 150,000. In 1832 it had increased to 263,554.[†] The period may be named as the age of newspapers,

---

[*] I have in this case to acknowledge my obligations to the Lieut.-Governor of Ontario, Hon. John Beverley Robinson, who has made great exertions to learn the first printed book of his province. The answers to the letters which he was good enough to write, he informs me, supply no information with regard to any publication anterior to that of Thompson, named in the text. Mr. Brymner, likewise, is unacquainted with any book prior to this work.

[†] Census of Canada, Ottawa, 1876, Vol. IV., pp. 83 and 112.

for the population, small as it was, was much scattered. York had but 5,500 inhabitants. There was little reward offered to the man of letters. He could become a schoolmaster or edit a country journal to receive the patronage or rebuke of some petty local celebrity : there was no other career open to him. But in all conditions of society, books are often published without hope of material benefit. There is a class of works which always finds a sale : School Books. One would fancy that some primer existed, some early Reader, that some Canadian Donatus* had left behind him a volume of this character : none has been found. The first published book in Toronto, is said to be by the late Bishop, when Archdeacon Strachan. Its title is, "A letter to the Congregation of St. James Church, York, Upper Canada, occasioned by the Hon. John Elmsley's publication of the Bishop of Strasbourg's observations on the 6th Chapter of

---

* The Donatus, so called from its editor or compiler, is one of the first of known books. It is an elementary school grammar printed from wooden blocks, before the introduction of moveable type. It has been stated also that a Donatus was the first example of typography of the date 1450. There is a tradition only to this effect, no copies are known. The first book with moveable type *with wood-cuts*, bears the date "Am Sant Valentinus tag 1461." It was printed at Bamberg, by Albert Pfister. Only one copy is known at the Wolfenbuttel Library, memorable as having been the place where Lessing acted as Librarian, and where Luther's Bible is preserved. Napoleon, who knew the impression which such matters make on the French mind, and who had a respect for all literary power, whatever form it took, preferring it, however, to be servile to his own views, carried off this book to Paris. After the campaign of one hundred days, and the surrender of the capital in 1815, this *unique* volume was claimed to be returned to the spot whence it had been taken, as if it had been a cession of territory with many thousand population. The Bible published at Metz, by Faust and Guttenburg, known as the Mazarine Bible, was printed either in 1455 or 1456. One of the "supposed earliest productions" of typography is a letter of indulgence, dated 12th August, 1451, by Pope Nicolas V. to Paulin Zappe, Ambassador of the King of Cyprus. It was probably printed in 1454.

St. John's Gospel, by John Strachan, D.D., LL.D., Archdeacon of York, &c., York. Printed by Robert Staunton, (no date on title page) 1834."* It is to be presumed that the Bishop of Strasbourg's observations were printed elsewhere.†

---

* I have to acknowledge my obligations to Mr. Frank Joseph, of Toronto, to whom I am indebted for this rare pamphlet.

† The earliest book on Upper Canada known to the writer is "A Short Topographical Description of His Majesty's Province of Upper Canada, in North America, to which is annexed a Provincial Gazetteer, London, 1799." The following remarks are appended, "The accompanying Notes and Gazetteer were drawn up by David William Smyth, the very able Surveyor-General of the Province of Upper Canada, at the desire of Major-General Simcoe, on the plan of those of the late Captain Hutchins for the River Ohio and countries adjacent."

This work is invaluable for its statistical information with regard to the Province at that date. The first edition is rare; the only one known to the writer is in the library of the Abbé Vérrault. The copy in the Parliamentary Library at Ottawa is the second edition revised and corrected by **Francis Gore**, Esq., Lieutenant-Governor, &c., &c. 8vo. London, 1813.

At this date another Mr. Smith, (M.) brought out a volume on the same subject. The title of his first edition, published in Hartford, Connecticut, 1813, is: "A Geographical View of the Province of Upper Canada and promiscuous remarks on the Government, in two parts, with an Appendix containing a complete description of the Niagara Falls and remarks relative to the situation of the inhabitants respecting the war." The second edition, published in Baltimore in 1814, has for title, "A Geographical View of the British possessions in North America comprehending Nova Scotia, New Brunswick, New Britain, Lower and Upper Canada, with all the country to the Frozen Sea to the North, and Pacific Ocean to the West."

Mr. M. Smith tells us in his preface that in 1812 he had obtained permission of Lieut.-Governor Gore to publish the volume, when war was declared by the United States Government. Being a citizen of the Republic, and not being willing to take the oath of allegiance, he obtained passports for his own country. His MSS. having been taken from him before he left Canada, he was driven to supply their place from his rough notes.

One is somewhat puzzled to explain the publication of the volume under such conditions at this date, unless on the theory that it was felt by

It is not easy to find precise information as to the actual dates of many of the early newspapers. These newspapers are yet to be collected in the Archive Office. The Library at Ottawa, as well as the Legislative Library at Toronto, is quite destitute of authorities. It may be explained with regard to the Parliamentary Library at Ottawa that much of its contents of this character was destroyed in the fire of Montreal during the Rebellion Losses agitation in 1849, and in the two subsequent fires at Quebec. Works of this character are with difficulty replaced. The writer can, therefore, only follow on the beaten track.

According to Mr. MacMullen*, the second paper published was the *Upper Canada Guardian*, in 1807, which was started in opposition to the Government paper which attacked Judge Thorpe. The difficulty, to-day, is to understand the merits of the dispute between himself and Governor Gore. It is the fashion to trace the difficulty to the influence of the Family Compact Party.

Mr. Francis Gore arrived in Upper Canada in August, 1808. No one will pretend that any such party, which was afterwards known as the Family Compact, in any way then existed. It is precisely in the case of a matter of this character that the Archive Office will prove its use. There is nothing really to show whether Gore or Thorpe was right. But what would we say, to-day, if some Judge of one of Her Majesty's Courts of Justice took a prominent part in politics and became an agitator even in the mildest form. It is true

---

the publishers that is was necessary to give some information concerning the country to the north so soon to be a prey to the conqueror ! These volumes are curious and not without information. New Britain it may be said, was the name then given to that part of Labrador between the 59° and 65° degrees of Longitude.

* History of Canada, Brockville, 1868.

there was no law, except that of decency and propriety, against Judge Thorpe seeking a constituency. One would think of Burke's description of Wilkes, applying to the ermined candidate for a seat in Parliament, the Horatian Ode to Pindar (iv. 2.) :

numerisque fertur
Lege solutus;

Nor was Judge Thorpe fortunate in his editor, Willcocks. The latter died a colonel in the United States service at the attack on Fort Erie, having deserted the service of his country *during the war*, for he fought on the Canadian side at Queenstown.

In 1820, Mr. John Carey established the *Observer* at (York) Toronto. It existed, Dr. Scadding tells us, to about the year 1830.

The *Canadian Freeman* was established by Mr. Francis Collins, in 1825. The editor is named in the political history of that day as suffering from imprisonment for libel on the late Chief Justice Robinson in 1828. After Sir John Colborne's arrival, in 1829 the Assembly petitioned him to pardon Collins. Sir John Colborne, who had much of the military genius of the Duke, must have felt that his master's mode of speech was as equally worthy of admiration as his powers in the field : at least, the words of Lord Seaton so suggest : " I regret exceedingly that the House of Assembly should have made an application to me which the obligation I am under to support the laws and my duty to society, forbid me to comply with." The House, however, was equal to the occasion, it passed a resolution to the effect that they merited no such reproof.

These, however, were not the days when the press had much countenance, for in 1820, Mr. Ferguson, editor of the *Canadian Spectator*, was condemned to be imprisoned 18 months, to stand in the pillory, to pay a fine of £50, to find security for good behaviour for seven years, his own for £500, and two for £250.

Mr. Lindsey, in his "Life of Mackenzie," gives us full information of the literary efforts of that extraordinary man.* His first paper, the *Colonial Advocate*, was published at Queenstown, 18th May and was continued until 18th Nov., 1824. His opponents accused him of printing it at Lewiston, in the United States, across the river. It re-appeared in York, **25th** May, 1825. There was no issue from 16th June to 18th December, 1825. It was published to the 8th June, 1826, when the mob destroyed the types and presses. Mr. Mackenzie **sued the** parties who had been prominent in the **riot and received** £625 damages which, to use Mr. Mackenzie's **words**, re-established on a permanent footing *The Advocate* press. From the 25th January, 1827, to 10th January, 1828, Mr. Mackenzie styled himself "Printer to the Honorable House of Assembly of Upper Canada." The paper remained under Mr. Mackenzie's control until 4th of November, 1834, **when the** last number of the *Colonial Advocate* appeared.

---

* **During** the year 1885, the writer frequently met the late Sir **Francis Hincks**, whose melancholy death from small-pox was so painfully felt. Among **other** places, at the well-known publisher's, Mr. Drysdale, and at the City Club. The void he has left in that circle is known only to those who attended it, a void so soon to be felt after that of the late estimable Mr. Thomas Cramp On nearly the last occasion which the writer saw him, 10th April, the conversation turning upon Sir Francis' lately published book, "Reminiscences of his Life," he told the writer that, as the position of the Toronto Postmaster became vacant, being then in power, he offered it to Mackenzie, considering that it would be a respectable provision for his declining years. Sir Francis adding that whatever criticism might be made upon Mackenzie, he certainly had not sought to enrich himself. The offer was declined, Mackenzie entertaining the feeling that the Government desired to purchase his silence, as Sir Francis added, "Certainly our last thought." The position was given to Mr. Leslie.

The press and type were sold to Dr. O'Grady, a Roman Catholic ecclesiastic, then resenting some injustice from the higher authorities of his Church. The *Advocate* was incorporated with *The Correspondent* and the new journal was called *The Correspondent and Advocate.*

Subsequently, Mr. Mackenzie published the first number of the *Constitution* on the 10th July, 1837, the last number was published on the 29th November. Mr. Lindsey tells us: Vol. I., page 390, "The first and fourth page of the number for December 6th were printed when at this stage it was brought to a violent close by the breaking out of the insurrection. The forms and type were broken up by the loyalist mob."

The labours and career of Mr. Gourlay were prior to this date. His letters commenced about 1818, many were written to the *Niagara Spectator* and copied into the *Kingston Gazette.* His work in Canada, "General Introduction to the Statistical Account," appeared in London, in 1822. Subsequently, in Boston, in 1844, he published the *Neptunian.* The writer had seen but four numbers of this paper, 23 to 26, until he was shown among the Archives, a bound volume of Nos. 1 to 12 having the author's autograph. They are without date. But the contents establish the date, which he has assigned them. In No. 25 Mr. Gourlay gave "Correspondence after leaving Home for Canada," in which he included many letters (1817 and 1820) to and from his wife, which men do not generally publish themselves, whatever may be done after their death. It is believed that this publication is rare. His career in Canada was as unfortunate to the reputation of others as to himself. A Scotchman, he was imprisoned as an alien, as a seditious person brought within the meaning of a Statute passed in 1804. A writ of *habeas corpus* was granted, but bail was refused. The Act which gave the warrant to these arbitrary and discreditable proceedings was repealed two years after this event. Mr. Gourlay's name has a place in the political, rather than the literary history of the country, although in the latter point of view it can in no way be justly omitted.

The works by which Mr. Gourlay will be known and remembered are :

General introduction to the statistical accounts of Upper Canada compiled with a view to a grand system of emigration, London, 1822.

Statistical Account of Upper Canada, 2 vols, London, 1822.

Among the books published at this date mention may be made of :

"A View of the Political Situation in the Province of Upper Canada, in N. A., in which her physical capacity is stated ; the means of diminishing her burden, increasing her value, and securing her connection to Great Britain, are fully considered, by John Mills Jackson, 1809."

By Sir Richard Bonnycastle :

"Excursions in Canada, or Canada in 1841," 2 vols., 1841, London.

"Canada in 1846," 2 vols.

"Canada as It Was, Is, and May Be," edited, with considerable additions, by Sir James Alexander, 1852.

"Canadiana, containing sketches of Upper Canada, and the crisis in its political affairs, by W. B. Wells, 1837."

"The Life of Colonel Talbot, and the Talbot Settlement," by Mr. Edward Ermatinger, was published at St. Thomas, in 1859.

Several newspapers appeared from time to time in different parts of the Province, and the information regarding them can only be imperfectly given. Many of these journals have passed away, and are forgotten, except when named in allusion to some past event. Some few exceptions are yet in existence. It has been found difficult to meet the early copies which alone establish the date of commencement. The above dates are given without guarantee for precision.

The *Kingston Gazette*, weekly, was established in 1810, by Mr. Myles. It was continued until 1818. In 1819 the paper appeared under the name of the *Kingston Chronicle*. It was afterwards called the *Chronicle and Gazette*. Finally, in 1840, it became known as the *Chronicle and News*.

The *Kingston, Upper Canada, Herald* was established 1819, by Mr. Hugh C. Thompson.

The Kingston *Watchman* appears to have been published between 1822-33.

The *Patriot* appeared in 1829, under Mr. Dalton. The number seen is Vol. I., No. 51, 26th October, 1830.

The *Spectator* was published in 1830. It was edited, at one time, by Dr. Barker.

The *Catholic Religious Weekly Periodical* was published in Kingston, from Oct. 22, 1830, to Oct. 14, 1831, by Vicar-General McDonald.

The *British Whig* was established in 1834. It appeared as a daily paper in 1849. It was the property of Dr. Barker.

The above are all of Kingston.

At Toronto, the *Christian Guardian*, the organ of the Methodists, is still in existence. The first number is dated 13th November, 1829.

The *Patriot and Farmers' Monitor*, edited by Mr. Dalton, commenced in 1829, at Kingston, was subsequently transported to Toronto. It may be recollected of late years in connection with the *Leader*.

The *Courier*, edited by Mr. George Gurnet, was commenced the beginning of December, 1829. The last number appeared in March, 1837 ; the date when Mr. Gurnet was elected Mayor of Montreal, and was appointed by Sir F. B. Head, Clerk of the Peace for the Home District.

The *Examiner* was established by Sir Francis Hincks at the commencement of his career, early in July, 1838, and passed from his hands to the control of Mr. Leslie. In 1857 the subscription list was sold to Mr. Brown, and was merged in that of the *Globe*. The first number of the *Globe*, however, appeared 5th March, 1844.

The *Brockville Recorder* was started in 1820, and immediately passed into the hands of Mr. Buel, who retained control of it until 1849, when it was transferred to Mr. Wylie. In 1883, it became the property of the present owner, Mr. J. J. Bell.

The *Prescott Telegraph* was commenced in 1823 by Mr. Myles who, in 1810, had started the *Kingston Gazette*.

The first By-town paper was the *Independent*, started in 1837 by "Jimmy" Johnston, the eccentric member for Carleton. After a few numbers it became extinct, to pass into the hands of Dr. A. J. Christie, who re-established it as the *Bytown Gazette*. This paper, after passing through several ownerships, was finally discontinued in 1862.

The *Cornwall Observer* was started in 1834.

The *Traveller*, or *Prince Edward Gazette*, appeared at Pictou in 1836. It lived four years.

The *Anglo-Canadian* was published at Belleville, in 1831. The paper was short-lived. It was succeeded by the *Phœnix*, which was published for about a year.

In 1834 the *Belleville Intelligencer* was established. It is now in existence.

The *Port Hope Telegraph* was established in 1831.

The *Reformer* appeared in Cobourg in 1832.

The *Brantford Sentinel* was published in 1837. The first attempt was a failure. It was subsequently successfully renewed by Mr. Thorpe Holmes.

The *Gore Balance* was published in Hamilton in 1830. The *Western Mercury* in 1831.

The first number of the *Saint Catharines' Journal* appeared 1st Feb., 1826, published by Hiram Leavenworth. In 1843 it was transferred to Mr. Thorpe Holmes, who controlled it until 30th June, 1857. It is still in existence.

Doubtless, there were many attempts more or less successful in the line of journalism which remain unrecorded. There is no attempt in these pages in any way to give a complete list of such efforts, or even to affect accuracy as to dates. Much which has been published on the subject has often been carelessly put to paper without the least sense of responsibility, and without any assurance of correctness of statement. No one could imagine the difficulty of tracing an early number of a newspaper fifty or sixty years back until he went in search of it. Such list, no doubt, is attainable. Possibly the imperfections of what is here deferentially offered, may lead many young men in the several cities and towns, correctly to supplement the information so imperfectly given, and it can best be done by a division of labour, for the investigations will exact time and effort.

It would be conceived that Corporations would make it a matter of duty to gather for reference of the community, complete fyles of all newspapers published in the locality, together with all books which have been written to describe the history and traditions of the place. The commercial and legal value of such a proceeding must be admitted. The obligation could be made a special duty attached to the position of the city clerk, many of the incumbents of which office are men of literary ability. The difficulty has hitherto been, that there has been a general indifference in this respect. Frequently, even, it is not possible to obtain a copy of an old repealed By-law. No doubt the very idea in keeping this record may be new to many; nevertheless a little reflection will show the utility of the proceeding. It is yet time, in many localities, to supply this defect, with but little trifling expense a commencement may be made in the collection of the archives of each municipality. No Mayor ought to be allowed to divest himself of responsibility in this respect. It should be a special matter with the city clerk annually to report on the steps taken during the year. When the collection has once been established on a proper basis the expense will be limited to a few dollars to bind the newspapers received and in purchasing the few books which annually appear.

So trifling is the whole proceeding that it is a matter of wonder that it has not been attended to.

The truth must be said that Ontario Archæology is so little in its first stage. Of late years it has received no slight impulse from the efforts of Dr. Scadding, whose "Toronto of Old" is well-known, and who continues his research with system and care. His endeavour is to obtain original authorities, to base his narrative on solid evidence, rejecting that easy and convenient principle of acceptance of a repeated, unauthenticated fact. We are commencing to recognize the necessity of studying our annals, in order to penetrate the surface of tradition. A marked consequence of this feeling is shown on the walls of Government House. Within the last few years, with some few exceptions, the portraits of the Lieut.-Governors of Upper Canada, with the Administrators of the Government, have been ranged side by side* and have attracted the attention of all who have participated in the hospitalities so gracefully dispensed during the tenure of office of the present Lieutenant-Governor. That the writer can at all speak of the subject is due to the kindness of Governor Robinson. Few who look upon these portraits can form any idea of the patient labour by which the satisfactory results have been achieved. It can be well understood as one sees the many letters which the search has necessitated. And those portraits which are absent have been among those which have led to the greatest amount of correspondence. Mr. Robinson has made a life-long study of the early history of Upper Canada, and, together with the circumstance that from his early boyhood in his father's house, he has met the leading actors in our politics, for some years beyond a half century, he felt that the opportunity of obtaining some record of them should not be allowed to pass. The proposition made to the head of the Government, Mr. Mowat, obtained his warm sympathy and support. The Council agreed to provide for the expense on a reasonable and proper basis, and proceedings were at once taken to carry out the design. It can easily be understood that it was one thing to agree to obtain a series of painted portraits; and that it is an entirely different matter to carry out the theory. The last of these portraits, that of Sir George Arthur, dates nearly half a century back. The first goes back to beyond nearly double this period. The starting point to be determined is where any particular portrait can be found, and in the second place to obtain permission to copy it. This multifarious correspondence was carried on

---

*The original portraits and copies have been made with care and ability by Mr. Berthon, known in Toronto as the artist who painted the several portraits of the Chief Justices and Chancellors in Osgoode Hall, Toronto. Mr. Berthon was a pupil of his father, the Court Painter of the First Napoleon. A portrait of the Emperor, taken from life by the elder Berthon, still remains in the possession of his son.

by the Lieutenant-Governor with several of the parties to be addressed. A great extent of the necessary investigation was conducted by his brother, Colonel Charles Robinson, of the Rifle Brigade, who has been indefatigable in his inquiries, and, as a rule, successful, although it will be seen that in some rare instances success is yet to be hoped for. The Province is under very great obligations to Colonel Robinson for the zeal and judgment with which this service has been rendered. Accepting Governor Robinson as an authority, the Governors of Ancient Upper Canada are as follows:—

General Simcoe	8 July,	1792.
Peter Russell, President, Administrator	21 July,	1796.
General Peter Hunter	17 Aug.,	1799.
Alex. Grant, President, Administrator	11 Sept.,	1805.
Francis Gore	25 Aug.,	1806.
Sir Isaac Brock, President	30 Sept.,	1811.
Sir Roger Hale Sheaffe	20 Oct.,	1812.
Baron de Rottenburgh	19 June,	1813.
Sir Gordon Drummond (Provisional Lieut.-Governor.)	13 Dec.,	1813.
Sir George Murray	25 April,	1815.
Sir Fred. Philipse Robinson	1 July,	1815.
Francis Gore	25 Sept.,	1815.
Col. Sam. Smith, Administrator	11 June,	1817.
Sir Peregrine Maitland	13 Aug.,	1818.
Col. Sam. Smith, Administrator	8 March,	1820.
Sir Peregine Maitland	30 June,	1820.
Sir John Colborne	5 Nov.,	1828.
Sir Francis Bond Head	25 Jan.,	1836.
Sir George Arthur	.. March,	1838.
Lord Sydenham { Arrived at Quebec, 17th Oct., 1839, Sworn at Toronto, }	21 Nov.,	1839.

Of the above, the portraits not obtained are those of General Peter Hunter, Alex. Grant, Sir Roger Sheaffe, Baron de Rottenburgh.

Although the portrait of Sir George Arthur is not yet upon the walls, full arrangements have been made to obtain it. The query naturally arises as to the genuineness of these portraits. It is an old trick of a class of dealers to christen an oil painting, especially when the picture is one of merit. The portrait passing for that of Hampden* is a case in point.

There is no fact of any kind to shew that it is authentic. Frequently, in good faith, a portrait becomes misnamed.

---

*The engraved portraits of Hampden are described in Granger's Biographical History of England (5th ed., 1824), Vol. iii., p. 5:

"JOHANNES HAMPDEN, vindex libertatis. *Audran Sc. De picta tabella apud virum illustrem Richardum Ellys, Baronettum; H. Sh. In Peck's ' Life of Milton.'* "

" JOHN HAMDEN (sic) ; *in armour Houbraken Sc.* 1740, *Illust. Head.* This is not from the same picture as the above, which represents him younger."

Mr. Granger adds the following note :

"It does not appear that there is any authentic picture of Hamden (sic). Sir Richard Ellys is said to have bought an old painting at a stall, and called it by his name. The late Mr. Hollis told me that he has made particular inquiry after a genuine portrait of him to have it engraved, and that he could never find an undoubted original."

In the edition above named, a note on authority of Mr. Bindley, is added :

"At Hampden House, in Bucks, there is a small bust of him in ivory, well-executed and supposed to have been done in his life ; it exhibits a thin, long-visaged man with whiskers." Vol. iv. of the Literary History of Mr. John Nichols, 1822, is dedicated to the memory of Mr. Bindley, one of His Majesty's Commissioners of Stamps, whose portrait is given as a fronti-piece. He was a bibliographer, and known collector of great research.

The above statement, the writer humbly conceives, not only justifies, but dictates the necessity of thoroughly establishing the genuineness of the national portraits gathered together by the Lieutenant-Governor of Ontario.

Often there is a lack of evidence to establish authenticity. A case of this character is now in archæological circles attracting some notice. At the close the war of 1812-15, the Legislature of Upper Canada voted a sword to Colonel Robinson, no Christian name being given. The late Chief-Justice Sir John Beverley Robinson was a lieutenant at Queenstown, honourably mentioned in the General's despatch. His elder brother was Peter Robinson, who founded Peterborough (about 1824) City and County, which are named after him. He was at Detroit with Brock, and was commissioned to bring General Hull, after the capitulation to Toronto. He died unmarried. But there is no knowledge of this sword in his family, nor can the Colonel Robinson be identified. It has been surmised that it is this Mr. Peter Robinson who held rank in the Canadian Militia. But no one living knows anything of the presentation. Nor is there the least tradition to establish to whom this sabre was given.

Governor Robinson has added to the many obligations under which he has placed the writer by giving direct information as to the sources of these several portraits, so that their genuineness is indisputable.

The portrait of Governor Simcoe is taken from a miniature in oils, presented to Revd. Dr. Scadding, by Captain Simcoe, son of the General.

The portrait of Peter Russell is taken from the original life-size given by Mr. Russell, himself, to Dr. Baldwin. It is now in the possession of Mr. Wilcox Baldwin, son of the Hon. Robert Baldwin.

No portrait has been obtained of Governor Peter Hunter, although no little effort has been made to gain information regarding him. Some of the biographies have attributed to him a relationship to the celebrated surgeon John Hunter, from the fact that the monument in the

Protestant Cathedral, Quebec, was erected by a doctor of that name. The family relationship is without foundation. Dying in Quebec, in 1805, he is lost to our history. Possibly these few remarks may attract attention to the fact of our want of knowledge regarding him. Any one who can aid in filling this gap in our archives will deserve the public thanks. The Governors-General at this period were Lord Dorchester and General Prescott. It is not impossible that their papers will throw light on the subject.

The portrait of Governor Gore is from a life-size painting given by him to his god-daughter, Miss Givens, sister to the Revd. Salter Givens. This lady is still living unmarried. The original remaining in her possession, it was thought, too, in view of its being required in the public interest, Miss Givens, might be induced to part with it, and the Executive were prepared to recognize its value. A friend was commissioned to approach the owner with all delicacy. But a slight allusion to such a proceeding shewed how extremely distasteful it would prove, and no further steps were taken.

The portrait of Col. Samuel Smith is copied from the original in the possession of the family still residing at Toronto. It is that of a young man in the uniform of the Rangers. None could be obtained of a later date.

Sir George Murray, one of the most distinguished of the Peninsular officers, at once left Canada, on hearing that Napoleon had again entered France. His portrait is taken from the portrait by Sir Thomas Lawrence. The painting is well-known to collectors from the engraving of Henry Mayer, published by Welch & Gwynne, in 1841. It is lettered "Major-General George Murray, Quarter-Master General of the Army in Spain and Portugal."

The portrait of Sir Gordon Drummond is copied by permission of his daughter, Lady Effingham, now living in Eaton Place, London. The original was life-size, and her ladyship most courteously gave every assistance to the Province in its endeavour to obtain a copy. Sir Gordon Drummond spoke of Canada as his native country. He was, indeed, a native Canadian, having been born either in Quebec or in Montreal, in 1771, when his father was Paymaster-General to the forces.

Sir Frederick Philipse Robinson, first cousin of Sir John Beverley Robinson, was a general officer of great distinction, and was of a Virginia family. His portrait was obtained from his daughter, Mrs. Hamilton, now living.

The portrait of Sir Peregrine Maitland, is enlarged from a cabinet picture in the possession of his son, General Maitland, Governor of the Tower of London.

The portrait of Sir John Colborne is taken from the life-size picture in the Hall of Upper Canada College, of which he was the founder.

Sir Francis Bond Head* is taken from the well-known engraving of him published some years back.

Sir George Arthur's portrait is not yet obtained, but every arrangement has been completed to gain possession of it through his daughter, Lady Bartle Frere, who fully acknowledges the desire of the Government to place her father's memory in the position it can claim. Her letter,

---

* According to Sir Francis Bond Head, the practice of hoisting the standard at Government House, and at the official place of reception in town when the Governor is present, originated with him. He tells us in his extraordinary "Narrative," (London, 1839) p. 110 : "In proportion as the Constitutionalists were observed to rally round the British flag (which I hoisted for the first time in the history of the Province on the roof of the Government House), &c., &c.

granting Governor Robinson's request, is a model of feminine and filial delicacy.

The portrait of Brock has been left to the last, because, hitherto, it has been considered that it was impossible to obtain any such memorial. His life was written by his brother-in-law, Mr. Tupper, as he himself, of an ancient Guernsey family, and, in speaking of this subject, p. 341, Mr. Tupper says:—

"The officers of the 49th, subscribed for a portrait of Brock for their mess room, and instructed their regimental agent to obtain it. The agent applied to the family for a copy, but, unfortunately, they possessed no good likeness of the General."

Major Richardson, in his "War of 1812," states, p. 68:

"As no portrait, public or private, of General Brock seems to have been preserved in this country, it may not be unimportant hereto give a slight written sketch of the hero: In person he was tall, stout and inclining to corpulency; he was of fair and florid complexion, had a large forehead, full face, but not prominent features, rather small greyish-blue eyes, with a very slight cast in one of them, small mouth, with a pleasing smile and good teeth. In manner he was exceedingly affable and gentlemanly, of a cheerful and social habit, partial to dancing, and although never married extremely devoted to female society. Of the chivalry of his nature and the soundness of his judgment, evidence has been given in the foregoing pages to render all comment thereon a matter of supererogation."

This fact may explain why the portrait is taken in profile. It was with this discouraging theory that the Lieutenant-Governor started in his endeavour to obtain intelligence of a portrait. A large packet of letters is the evidence of the unflagging enthusiasm and zeal, which led to success. Never were such qualities more judiciously exercised, and in this case, as in the others, the Province is under great obligations to Colonel Robinson, who was untiring in his labours, for such really they may be called. Finally, it was known, through Mrs. DeLisle, a niece of Brock, and the one member of the family surviving who was living when he fell, that there were two portraits of him, one held by Mrs. Huish, and one by Mrs. Tupper, widow of the author of his life, and the daughter of his sister. Both have been copied for the Government. The likeness is in profile. There is a theory that there was some scar or mark on the face which suggested the choice of this position.

This correspondence has been placed at the disposal of the writer. There cannot be a doubt that the likeness is a family picture, genuine, and admitted to be a likeness. As it often happens, some of the family were displeased with it, and it is not improbable that such was the case with Brock himself. There is nothing, however, directly to warrant this remark, but such is a fair inference from what is said, especially that it was not considered a good portrait. Among the letters of this correspondence, there is one from the daughter of Mrs. Tupper, which throws light on this point, and which, itself, is of unusual interest.

I trust that it will not be considered a breach of propriety in making public the following letter, for it is really of historical importance. The veneration felt in Canada for the memory of the illustrious Brock, is general in every sense. His name is a household word with our youth, and it will be a matter of common satisfaction to know that the portrait we possess is genuine and undoubted. The reason that this letter is selected for publication in preference to many others, will be apparent upon its perusal. It will strike a chord of sympathy in every Canadian heart, and the deep feeling which marks the text, the writer of the letter may be assured, will in no way be vulgarized by its publication. The letter is published without the permission of the writer. Unfortunately, there is not the time at our disposal to ask this permission. It is hoped that the

G

explanation will be accepted, and that the irregularity in giving to the world this knowledge of Brock will be lost sight of in the universal satisfaction with which that which is so well written will be accepted :

"GUERNSEY, January 25, 1882.

"My cousin, Mrs. LeCocq, brought me your letter of January 16th to read, in order that I might help her in answering your question. It occurred to my mother and to myself that you might wish to have a copy of my dear father's life and correspondence of Sir Isaac Brock, in order that you may yourself see what is there told relative to the various points you allude to. My cousin will have been able from the foot-note at p. 341* to explain that the reason why the 49th Regiment failed to procure a portrait of Sir Isaac was not that there was no existing likeness, but that there was *no good one*. She will also have told you that we never heard of a medal for Queenstown ; that for Detroit has been for many years in our possession, my father being the eldest son of the General's eldest sister, not one of Sir Isaac's nine brothers having left a son. We have also the coat in which he was killed, the handkerchief stained with his blood, and, I believe, every scrap of paper relating to him, for my father was an intense hero worshipper, and his gallant uncle was his chief hero. From my cradle I was taught every interesting particular concerning my great uncle, and Detroit and Queenstown have always been household words in our home. The last copy of the "Life" which I gave away was to the late lamented Dean Stanley, who had made so many inquiries about Sir Isaac after a visit to Canada, that I ventured, when he visited Guernsey, to send him the book. He wrote

---

*Vide page No. 96.

a much valued note, saying that 'ever since he saw the monument of Sir Isaac Brock on the Heights of Queenstown, below Niagara Falls, he had felt great curiosity about him, which curiosity would now be gratified.'

"You will see, by my signature, that I am an unworthy namesake of the "charming girl" of whom Sir Isaac writes, my dear father's fondly-loved eldest sister.

"Believe me, my dear Sir,
"Truly yours,
"HENRIETTA TUPPER."

It is evident that the Dominion has finally established an important department, that of Archives ; that its maintenance has become a matter of parliamentary faith, and that yearly a vote of money will lead to its development and increase : One additional requirement is now necessary, to find proper quarters where the treasures which have been collected will be available. They are now placed in three fire-proof rooms communicating one with the other, in the basement of the Western Departmental Block, Ottawa, crowded with bookshelves, which have to be multiplied in the most dexterous, and artistic manner, in order to find room where the books can be placed. It is almost an impossibility for the historical student to continue his researches there. Such a spot is unfit for the purposes it undertakes to satisfy. What is required is a building apart, carefully constructed, fire-proof, with a reading-room. A matter of cost of some $15,000. To use the slang of the day, the investment will pay. Strangers visiting Ottawa will include the Archives-room as one of the sights, for the Department is one *per et in se*, and has been prudently made distinct from the library. No book is permitted out of its precincts, so it can set at defiance the most enterprising Member of Parliament : and the devastations on the books in the library, and the losses of valuable volumes, shew what is possible in that direction. The visitor, seeing the wants and requirements of this institution, may remember that he may have something in the shape of an ancient book or a record to contribute, and thus our Archives will become, day by day, richer and more complete. This is no dream of a sanguine nature, hoping against hope. It is the teaching of experience. The first condition of the Archive Department is to make it known, to bring it to public notice, and so silently appeal for support, aid, and encouragement.

One name particularly is deserving of mention in the establishment of this Institution, it is that of Dr. J. C. Taché, Deputy Minister of Agriculture, himself a student of the ancient remains of Canada, and one who has followed the history of the Dominion. It was fortunate that the establishment of this branch took place under his rule. With literary tastes, a practised writer, one whose life has been passed in investigation, he knew well what is needed in an organization the object of which is to gather sound and reliable information. No better man could have been found to have encouraged and to have sustained Mr. Brymner, in the duties he has so admirably fulfilled, and Dr. Taché has, in this respect, a firm and permanent claim on public gratitude.

Cui bono—to the benefit of what principle or interest, says pert and prosperous ignorance, that cursed Old Man of the Mountain, now astride on the shoulders of Canada, *Cui bono*—what is all this expenditure of time and money? Heaven help us if we are ever to be what we are to-day, weighed down by the theory that money is everything, the one be-all and end-all of life, the one excellence of the Horatian axiom, in comparison with which everything *vilior alga est*. We have a youth rising up to maturity among us. We do not hope to see the mantle of many a sire descending on them. We look forward to the **acceptance** of broader and more generous theories of life, to a higher sense of duty than we hear expounded at this hour, to the sentiment of some chivalry, to sympathies higher and more catholic than that which mere sordid self-interest teaches. Beauty is truth—truth beauty, in the words of Keats, and as we introduce and make known among these following us the generous and nobler instincts of historic truth, and that which it indicates, the love of truth, we cultivate a higher order of morality and a more dignified sense of public duty. As we educate and elevate each succeeding generation, so we raise them in the standard of a sense of manhood and personal dignity. We make them men. We do not say that the Archives Office will evangelize society. But it may produce and turn in the right direction many a young mind **whose** honest impulses and labours hereafter may exercise **wide, lofty,** and happy influences. It may also produce many a **prig** and may lead disordered vanity to many a sorry exhibition. **The** words of Cowper rise to the writer's mind: **Cowper,** whose memory is so dear to every lover of pure, good English, and whose noble, unselfish nature has produced some of the most **undying** passages of our literature :

> Knowledge and wisdom, **far from** being one
> Have ofttimes no connection. Knowledge dwells
> In heads replete with thoughts of other men ;
> Wisdom in minds attentive to their own.
> Knowledge a rude unprofitable mass,
> The mere materials with which wisdom builds
> Till smoothed and squared and fitted to **its place,**
> Does but encumber whom it seems to enrich.
> Knowledge is proud that he has learned so much ;
> Wisdom is humble that he knows no more.

It is no exaggeration to hope for the most desirable consequences in the training of our youth, in the impulse thus given to our history. The progress made by those officially in charge of the archives has been very great. The directors of the institution are in every way deserving of public approbation. What, however, is the principal requirement is a proper building, as we have pointed out, where the application of our historical wealth may be put to good purposes, and no step in this branch of practical economy would be more welcome than the knowledge that a sum had been placed in the estimates to carry out the design of preserving the memorials of our history in a fit home. There should be no haste in hurrying through the completion of the building. Every requirement of the institution should be perfectly well considered, and every want cared for and supplied. The details of its arrangement should be thoroughly investigated, and the building should be as perfect as experience and consideration can make it.

NOTE.—The explanation that Kirke (see page 29) came to be considered a renegade Frenchman, is that writers have neglected to refer to the proper authorities on the subject. Kalm's Travels, published in 1772. correctly states the fact :

"In 1629, towards the end of July, it (Quebec) was taken by two *Englishmen*, *Lewis* and *Thomas* Kirk, by capitulation, etc." Vol. I., p. 200.]

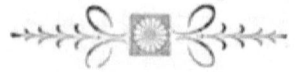

NOTE.

From sources the very opposite, the writer will endeavour to give an approximate list of the Ontario newspapers, as they were published in 1831. In that year, on the ground that the articles which appeared in *The Colonial Advocate* were libels on the House of Assembly, Mr. W. Lyon Mackenzie, then a member, was expelled on a vote of 24 to 15. These "libels" are given by his son-in-law, Mr. Lindsey, in the history of his life. There can only be a feeling of wonder that they should excite more than passing anger; and it is impossible to avoid admitting the justice of the remark so often made that the dominant party were determined to crush all opposition which threatened their tenure of power. It is not, however, in these pages that that subject can be discussed. In his defence, Mr. Lyon Mackenzie said: "The newspaper press of this Colony takes different sides in political questions. Four-fifths of the *twenty-five journals published in this Colony*, &c., &c."

The question suggests itself, are we to accept this number, in a general way, as an approximation, or as a precise and definite statement. Anyone who studies Mr. Lyon Mackenzie's career and does him justice must incline to the latter. Much of his writing and his tone of argument is marked by abruptness, by want of continuity. Although Mr. Mackenzie, on some occasions, wrote good English, he was frequently led to be discursive. Much that he put to paper can be well described as coming under the French emphatic word *décousu*. But in any matter of fact, in any statement, however impulsive Mr. Mackenzie might be in his anger, and however marked his language, the impression made upon the writer is that he was guided by a love of truth, and was even careful in his facts. We, therefore, on his view, are justified in accepting the number 25 as the actual number of political journals at that date, not including purely religious dogmatical publications. This opinion is sustained by the Post Office reports, which throw light on the subject.

Even in an essay of this character one can speak of the Post Office of that date archæologically. For under whatever aspect it may be considered, it was about as depressing and unsatisfactory an institution as ever existed. It was under Imperial control, its local head for many years setting at defiance all Canadian interference, nearly up to the time of its transfer, 6th April, 1851: Mr. James Morris being the first Postmaster-General. It was run to pay. No manager of an itinerant show could have been actuated by more sordid and selfish principles, than that which marked its management. We are told in the "Second Report of a Special Committee of the House of Assembly of the Province of Lower Canada, on the subject of the Post-Office Department. Session, 1835-1836." "For the thirteen years, ending 1834 inclusive, the enormous sum of £91,685 8s. 8d. sterling ($446,525), has been transmitted to England by the Post Office of this Province." And at the time of the report, the remittance was £10,041 13s. 4d. ($49,433), an annual tax upon the intelligence of Canada sent out of the country. That such was the desire of any Imperial Statesman cannot for a moment be believed. So to consider, is unfair to the mind the least susceptible of the advance of improvement. The system grew up from the utter failure of those conducting the establishment to understand its responsibilities, and its duties, blended, doubtless, with the sentiment that the position of the leading officials was exceedingly lucrative and pleasant. The postage of a letter to and from England ranged, at one time, from a dollar to a dollar and a half. Even to the latest date of this rule, the Canadian rate was 9d. (15c.) the half ounce immediately reduced under Provincial control to 3d. or five cents. What we recognise as the public interest, in the early days, in no way came into consideration. No additional post office could be established without the authority of the Imperial Postmaster-General. The regulations regarding newspapers, almost prevented, certainly very much limited their circulation. Postage had to be paid in advance, and the rate was high; an impediment to the discussion of political questions, which certainly found no disfavour with the military governors formed in the school of the Regency and with the few men in power clustered around them. Towards the final working of the system it became improved. But it is astonishing that it was allowed to continue so long after the vicious character of the system had been freely recognized. Lord Durham, in his celebrated report, gives but a few lines to the Post Office, recommending its immediate transfer to the Canadas. The rebellion of 1837-8, may explain much of the forgetfulness into which the matter passed. Had Lord Sydenham lived, it would doubtless have been immediately changed. The political difficulties which followed his death, engrossed public attention to the exclusion of all other matters, and until their settlement no steps were taken to effect the change called for.

It is proper to remark that, even at this date, many acquainted with the Post Office history, contend that the condition in which the office was found half a century back was unavoidable. Mr. Stayner, they urge, was an able man, and his integrity above suspicion; the fact, indeed, is not disputed. They argue that there was no statute under which the Post Office could be worked otherwise. The Act which governed its arrangements was that of Queen Anne for the plantations, and, moreover, the several Provinces would in no way act in common to obtain a better system. The excess of revenue, it is contended, was made up to a great extent of the Imperial and Military Postage, which amounted to a large sum. It is, however, indisputable that the system was bad and mischievous, that it was controlled entirely by the Imperial authorities, and that it was in the power of the Home Government at any time to introduce the necessary reforms when they held it expedient to do so, and that no changes were made.

The country was indebted to Mr. Mackenzie that, in the first instance, any inquiry was made into its condition. Mr. Lindsey tells us that Lord Goderich proposed at once to place the Post Office under Provincial control, and offered the Ontario management to Mr. Mackenzie. The offer he felt bound to decline. Even, however, to have compassed such a reform was a sufficient epitaph.

Allusion has been made to a Special Committee of the Lower Canada House of Assembly in 1835-6 in the Post Office. Mr. Stayner was examined as a witness. The day had gone by when he could defy a Canadian House of Assembly. Among other matter he presented a return shewing in detail the postage received on newspapers during the five years from 1827-31. By availing ourselves of this information, and what incidental facts can be elsewhere obtained, it may be concluded that the following papers were in circulation at that date:

KINGSTON.—*Kingston Chronicle, Upper* **Canada** *Herald, Kingston* **Patriot,** *The Canadian Watchman, The* **Spectator.**

PRESCOTT.—*Prescott Telegraph.*

BROCKVILLE.—*Brockville Recorder, Brockville Gazette.*

BELLEVILLE.—*Anglo-Canadian.*

PERTH.—*Perth Examiner.*

PORT HOPE.—*Telegraph.*

COBOURG.—*Cobourg Star.*

TORONTO.—*Upper Canada Gazette, The Canadian Freeman, Colonial* **Advocate,** *The Christian Guardian, The Courier.*

YORK.—*York Observer.*

HAMILTON.—*Western* **Mercury, Free Press, Canadian Wesleyan.**

GORE.—*Gore Balance, Gore Gazette.*

NIAGARA.—*Niagara Gleaner.*

ST. CATHARINES.—*St. Catharines Journal.*

Total, 25.

INDEX.

	PAGE.
Abeille, Canadienne	39, 40
Abercrombie, General	18
Admiralty Law	26
Agnew, Mr. Stair	16
Alexander, Sir James	85
American Oracle, The	77
Ancien Conseil, Registres de. Where are They?	61
Anglo-American, The Belleville	87
Antell, Mr.	42
Archive Branch:	
Reports	11
Origin	12
Its Establishment,	100
Its Future Influence,	101
The Requirement of a Proper Building	102
Arrêt du Conseil, Education 1718	33
Arthur, Sir George. His Portrait	95
Aurore, L'	43
Aval, Mr.	16
Aylmer, Lord	48
Baby, Mr. Justice	41
Baldwin, Mr. Wilcox	93
Baldwin, Dr.	93
Bay of Quinte Mission	30
Bell, Mr. I. J.	87
Belleville Intelligencer	87
Belmont, M. L'Abbe. His History	46
Berthon, M., Painter, Portraits, Toronto	90
Bibaud, Jeune	41
Bibaud, M.	43
His History	48
His Career	49
Reproof of *barguignage*	49
Bibliothèque Canadienne, La	43
Binding—	53
Earliest Example	54

	PAGE.
Blanchet, Mr.	50
Blanchet, Mr., 1884	60
Board of Trade, London	15
Bonnycastle, Sir Richard. His Works	85
Boucher's Memorial to Colbert	44
Bouquet Papers	18
Bourdon, Jean	32
Bourgeois, Marguerite	33
Brantford Sentinel	88
British Flag, when first raised on Government House	95
British Population after Conquest	24
British Museum, The	15
British Whig, The	86
Brock, Sir Isaac, General :	
His Last Letter	18
His Portrait	96
Brockville Recorder	87
Brymner, Mr. Douglas	11
In London	15
In Montreal, etc.	17, 28
As to Documents relating to Quebec Act	38
Etymology, Toronto	74
Buckley, Captain	42
Buel, Mr.	87
Buies, Mr. Arthur, proposes "Le Dominion"	69
Burgoyne, General, Failure of	18
Supposed Influence Injurious to Carleton	19
His Character	19
His Surrender, Saratoga	19
Bytown Independent, The	87
Callières, M. de	46
Canada : Its struggles for existence as a British Province	37
Its Condition, 1765	24
Canadian Freeman	82
" *Magazine*	44
" *Review*	44
" *Spectator*	82
" Trade Act, 1822	58
Canadien, Le	39
Carleton, Sir Guy, Lord Dorchester	19
His Retirement	20

	PAGE.
Cartier, Sir George—Scene House of Commons	67
Catéchisme du Diocèse de Sens	41
Catherine, La Sainte	9
Catholic Religious Weekly Periodical	86
Carey, Mr. John	82
Celles, de, Mr.	53
Census, First, Murray	23
Chambre de Justice de Longueuil	59
Champlain	45
Edition of His Works	63
Charles I., Surrender of Canada, 1631	28
His Letter to Sir Charles Wake	29
Charlevoix	29, 33
His History	44, 46
Charon Frères	33
Chauveau, Mr. Sheriff	41, 67
Christian Guardian	86
Christie's History	50
Christie, Dr. A. J.	87
Civil Officers, Improper Choice after Conquest	25
Fault Remedied	38
Cobourg Reformer	88
Cochrane, Mr.	55
Colborne, Sir John, His Reply to an Address	82
His Portrait	95
Collins, Mr. Francis, Imprisoned for Libel	82
Colonial Advocate	83
Colonial Office	15
Intervention to Facilitate Search of Papers	15
Commercial Law, English	26
Conseil Souverain de Quebec	61
Constellation, The	77
Constitutional Act, The, 1791	19
Cornwall Observer	87
Cornwallis' Capitulation, 1781	22
Corporations, Duties of, with regard to Local Literature and Periodicals	88
Courier, The	87
Courier de Quebec, Le	39
Couture, le Sieur	32
Cramp, Mr. Thomas	83
Criminal Law, British, Unpopular with Seigneurs	27

		PAGE.
Dablon, Père		32
Dalhousie, Lord		7, 50
Attacks Press Against		50
Decrêts, Arrêts, Ordonnances		5
Departmental Room		12
Derby, Lord, 1776		20
" Translator of Homer		73
" (1883.)		16
Des Grosseliers		29, 32
Dictionnaire Généalogique des Familles Canadiennes		63
Detroit, Fort, Attack in 1764		28
Disney, Capt. 44th Regiment, his trial		23
Pamphlet of trial		41
Dixon, Mr. T.		16
Donatus		79
Drummond, Sir Gordon. His Portrait		95
Drysdale, Mr., Publisher		83
Du Calvet, M.		20
Possibly United States Partisan		22
Duchesneau, Intendant.		45
Du Luth, constructed Fort Kaministiquia, 1698		30
Education, Provision for, previous to Conquest		33
Encyclopédie Canadienne, L'		43
Epochs Lower Canada History.		41
Etablissement de la Foi.		45
Examiner, The.		87
Faillon, M. l'Abbé.		61
Faribault, Mr. G. B.		52
The importance of his labours		53
Ferguson, Mr.		82
His severe sentence for libel		83
Fees, Law, exorbitant character of.		26
Ferland, M. l'Abbé		61
First Book published Quebec		41
First Book published Montreal		41
First Book published Ontario		78
Fisher, Dr.		51
Fothergill, Mr.		77
Frazer, Dr.		16
Frazer, Captain, 1764		23

	PAGE.
Frederickton Papers	17
Free Press	42
French Canadian population :	
Described by Murray	24
Described by Kalm	34
Present composite in descent	64
View of, in London, 1760	71
French Canadian Volunteers, Detroit, said to be unjustly treated	28
Frontenac, Governor	45
Gage, General	19
Garnet, Mr.	16
Gayangoz, Pascual de	16
Gilmore, Thomas	35
Givens, Miss	94
Globe, The	87
Gore, Mr. Francis, Lieut.-Governor.	80, 81
His portrait	94
Gore Balance, The	88
Gosford, Lord	48
Gourlay, Mr. His Works	84
Grant, Mr.	38
Gregory, Mr.	42
Gurnet, Mr. George	87
Haldimand, Governor, appointed	19
His character	22
His difficult duties.	20, 22
Haldimand Papers.	18, 19
Haldimand House.	21
Halifax Documents.	17
Hall, Mr. Patterson	21
Hampden's Portrait, spurious	92
Hardy, Mr. W.	16
Hardwicke, Lord	26
Hayes Fort, Hudson's Bay, Attack on	31
Head, Sir Francis Bond. His Portrait	95
Heine-Heinrich, Early appreciation of the influence of Railways	8
Henry, Anthony	42
Herriott, History of Canada	46

	PAGE.
Hey, William, Chief Justice	42
Hincks, Sir Francis, his offer to W. Lyon Mackenzie refused,	83
The Examiner	87
Historical Society, Quebec, formation	7
Historical Society, Montreal	7
Histories of Canada	44
Holmes, Mr. Thorpe	88
Holton, Mr.	67
Home Government, desire to govern justly	26
Hôtel Dieu de Quebec, Histoire de	46
House of Assembly, Quebec, First Meeting	39
Hudson Bay—French expedition there, much of the account fabulous	29
Transactions between England and France, relative to, 1689	31
Hudson's Bay Co. papers	17
Hunter, Governor Peter, no portrait can be found. Not related to celebrated surgeon John Hunter, as stated	93
Jefferies' History French Dominions.	70
Jefferson, Thomas	37
Jesuit Relations	30, 44
Jesuit Journals	55
Jogues, Jesuit	30
Johnson, "Jimmy"	87
Joliet, le Sieur	30
Joseph, Mr. Frank	80
Judge, first appointed, taken from jail	25
Juchereau de l'Ignace, la Sœur	46
Kalm, Peter, description Canada Women	34
Kensington, Mr.	16
Kingston, Mr. Alfred	16
Kingston *Chronicle*	86
Kingston *Gazette*	86
Kingston *Upper Canada Herald*	86
Kingston *Watchman*	86
Kirke, an Englishman, not renegade Frenchman.	29, 102
Labrie, Dr. Jacques	52
Lambert's Travels	24
Lane, James	43
Latour, Mr.	41
Laval, Bishop	45
Memoirs of	46

	PAGE.
La Fontaine, Sir Hypolite, his contributions to Archæology	62
La Pointe Mission	30
La Salle	30, 45
La Tour, l'Abbé	46
La Vallière	32
La Verdière, l'Abbé, Editor Champlain's Works	63
Le Clerq, Christien	45
Letter, Mr. Parkman to Mr. Blanchet	60
L'Escarbot	45
Lee, Mr	50
Library, Ottawa, Loss of Books	13
Lieutenant-Governors Upper Canada, List of	91
Lindsay, Mr., of St. Johns, Loss of MS.	47
Lindsey, Mr. Charles, Life of Mackenzie	83
Literature, Slow Progress of	37
Lundy, Rev. F. J.	43
Lyons, Lord	16
Macculloh, Lewis Luke	42
Mackenzie, W. Lyon—His Newpaper—Refusal Postmastership Toronto	83
Magasin, Le, du Bas Canada	43
Magistrates after Conquest, Character of	25
Maitland Sir Peregrine. His Portrait	95
Marmette, Mr.	16
Marquette	30
Marriott, Mr. Advocate-General	38
Masères, Mr.	38, 42
His Career	51
Marshall, Mr.	16
Master of the Rolls	16
Munificent Gift of	17
McGill, Hon. Peter. His Portrait Destroyed	57
Memoires Historiques, Published by Quebec Government	60
Meade, Mr.	16
Medicine, Journal de, de Quebec	43
Mesplet, Fleury	40
Mezière, Mr. H.	39
Michipicoten	30
Military Correspondence, Extent of	13
Mississippi, Discovery of, 1673	30
Mondelet, Dominique	52

H

	PAGE.
Montmorency Falls	21
Montreal abuses Administration of Justice	27
" Documents	17
" *Aurore*	40
" *Gazette*	40
" *Herald*	40
" *Spectator*	40
Montizambert, Mr., late of Senate	44
Morrison, Mr.	42
Mowat, Mr., First Minister, Ontario	90
Murray, General—	19
On Walker affair	23
His despatch, 20th August, 1766	23
Description of Government	25
Performance of Duty	26
Myles, Mr.	86, 87
Neptunian, The	84
Newspapers, Early, Found with Diffitulty	86
New York Act 1767	37
Nova Scotia Chronicle	42
Nova Scotia Printing	42
Noyrot Père	45
Numismatic Society, Montreal	41
Observateur, l'	43
O'Grady, Dr.	84
Ontario Literary History	72
" Impulse given to Archæology by Portraits Government House	90
Ordinance, 1790, Preservation Ancient Documents	4
Overall, Mr.	16
Pamphlet Binding	53
Parkman Mr., of Boston, Historian	18, 60
Papet, Hessian Officer	21
Pasteur, C. B., Mr.	43
Patriot, The, and Farmers' Monitor	86
Payne, Capt., 1764, Committed for Contempt	23
Perrault, Joseph F. His History	48
Perrot, Nicolas	32
Phipps' Expedition, Repulse of	45

	PAGE.

Plamondon, **Louis**, Mr. .. 52
Plan of Code of Laws, Marriott .. 38
Plunkett, Mr. .. 16
Pontiac, Indian Chief .. 28
Poore, Mr. Perley .. 60
Port Hope *Telegraph* .. 86
Portraits City Hall, Montreal, Political Destruction of .. 57
Portraits Lieut.-Governors, Ontario, Record of their genuineness .. 92
Portraits often **Christened** by Dealers and Owners .. 92
Prescott *Telegraph* .. 87
Preston, Captain .. 37
Prevoté de Quebec Civils, Registres de la
    Are they rigorously kept? .. 61
    Necessity of Proper Editing .. 62
Prince Edward *Gazette* .. 87
Printing Unknown French Regime .. 24
Printing with Movable type, date first books .. 79
Puissance, **not** Recognized by Men of Education **as Proper**
    Translation for Dominion .. 66

Quebec Act, 1774 .. 19
    Described .. 20
Quebec Archæology .. 33
    " City of, taken by Kirke and restored by Charles I. .. 29
    " Documents .. 17
    " Provincial Limits Defined, 1764 .. 28
    " *Gazette* Established .. 35, 40
    " *Magazine* .. 39, 41
    " *Mercury* .. 40

Raddison .. 29, 32
    Asserted expedition **from Lake Superior to Hudson's Bay**,
    1667, an impossibility .. 29
Raymbault, Jesuit .. 30
Reclus, Onésime, Adopts **Translation "Le Dominion"** .. 69
Record Office, London— .. 15
    Few Canadian Documents there .. 18
Registres de l'Etat Civil .. 65
Registration, England, till 1836 .. 65
Registration, Dominion .. 66
Réglement de la Confrérie de l'adoration perpetuelle .. 41

	PAGE.
Regulations enforced, **Imperial offices**	15
Responsible Government, **first mention of**	73
Richardson, Major, on **General Brock's Portrait**	96
Riedesel, Major-General	21
Riedesel, Madame, **Memoirs**	21
Riellé, de, M.	16
Robinson, Col. Charles, Rifle Brigade. His efforts in England to obtain originals of Portraits of Lieut.-Governors	91
Robinson, Sir **Fred**. Philipse, Lieut.-Governor. His Portrait	95
Robinson, late Sir John Beverley	93
Robinson, **Hon. John** Beverley, **Lieut.-Governor, Ontario**	78
His collected Portraits of Lieut.-Governors of U.C.	90
His labours on the Collection	91
Robinson, Peter, founder of Peterborough	93
Robinson, Colonel, received Presentation of Sword, difficult to trace	93
Rupert, Fort	31
Russell, Peter. His Portrait	93
Ruthven, Mr.	54
Saberdache, **Mr. Jacques Viger**	57
Sabertache	57
Sagard, his History	45
Saint Catharines Journal	88
Sault St. Mary Mission	30
Meeting of Indians	32
Scribbler	42
Scadding, Dr., Toronto, **of Old**	89
Second Book Published, **Quebec**	42
Seminary, The Montreal	17
Sewell, Chief Justice	39
Spectateur Canadien, Le	43
Spectator, The	82
Shea, Mr., New York	44
Sherbrooke, Sir John Cope	56
Simcoe, Governor. His Portrait	76, 93
St. Lusson	32
Smith, Mr. M., Geographical View Province U.C., 1813	80
Smith, William, History of Canada	47
Smith, Col. Samuel, His Portrait	94
Smyth, David William, *Gazetteer U.C.*, 1799	80
Stanton, Mr.	77

	PAGE.
Strachan, Bishop, Author Second Published Book	79
Superior, Lake, 1667	30
Taché, Dr. J. C., his good service, Establishment of Archive Branch	100
Talon, le Sieur	30
Tanguay, l'Abbé, his Labours	63, 65
Tessier, Doctor Xavier	43
Thompson, David, History of late War, 1832, First book, Ont.	78
Thorpe, Judge	81
Toronto, its Urban Character	74
Toronto, Etymology of Name	74
Tory Opinion Powerful till 1830	73
Tower, London	18
Tracy's Arrival	30
Trois Rivières, La Gazette de	40
Troyes, Chevalier de	31
Trudeau, Touissant, 1769	59
Trudeau, Touissant, Deputy Minister of Railway, 1868	59
Tupper, Mr., on Sir Isaac Brock's Portrait	96
Tupper, Miss Henrietta, her Letter	98
United States Sympathisers of 1776	21
Early Difficulties with	36
Upper Canada Gazette	77
Upper Canada Guardian	81
Vérrault, L'Abbé	11, 15
His Library	53
His Kindness to Author	54
Viger, Jacques	48, 53
His Labors	54, 58
His Career	56
His "Saberdache"	57
Viger, Dennis B.	52
Vincent, Mr.	16
Von Eking Memoir of General Riedesel	21
Walker Affair, 1764	23, 42
Walsingham Lord, Report of	26
War Office, Imperial	13, 15
Documents of Value	18

	PAGE.
Wells, W. B., *Canadiana*	85
Western Mercury	88
Wilcocks, Samuel H., killed at Fort Erie	82
William Henry, Lake George	18
Wilson, Mayor of Montreal, his portrait	57
Wolfe	50, 51
Women, Canadian, French Regime	33, 34
Wylie, Mr.	87
Young, Mr.	39

www.ingramcontent.com/pod-product-compliance
Lightning Source LLC
Chambersburg PA
CBHW022142160426
43197CB00009B/1402